Sheet Metal Bible

Timothy Remus

Published by:
Wolfgang Publications Inc.
PO Box 223
Stillwater, MN 55082
www.wolfpub.com

Legals

First published in 2010 by Wolfgang Publications Inc.,
PO Box 223, Stillwater MN 55082

© Timothy Remus, 2010

ISBN number: 978-1-929133-90-1

Printed and bound in China.

Sheet Metal Bible

Acknowledgements

Putting this book together meant digging deep into the archives, which made me realize just how long I've been at this job, or obsession, or whatever it is.

A long time ago I was lucky enough to score a commission from Motorbooks writing a group of books with and about Boyd Coddington. One day Boyd suggested I visit Steve Davis, and that is where my acknowledgments, and all of my sheet metal books, really start.

It was Steve who made me understand the art, craftsmanship and problem solving that goes into sheet metal fabrication. With patience, Steve explained the basics. Shrinking, stretching, and how bucks and paper templates could be used to make the whole job go so much easier. During lunch one day Steve told a story that I've repeated many times, let me paraphrase..... "When I was a young man trying to learn how to shape sheet metal, I worked with an old-timer named Red. He was very generous in sharing with me what he knew, and if it weren't for him I probably wouldn't be a fabricator today. Red's gone now and I'm getting older. I have a responsibility to pass on to other people the information that Red gave to me. That's why I want to help you do these articles, it's my way of passing on this information."

If Steve got me started it was another California native, Ron Covell, who fed both my interest in sheet metal fabrication and my ability to produce a good fabrication book. Ron not only did numerous how-to sequences for me, he introduced me to a number of fellow fabricators, and one of those was Bruce Terry. If you buy an old, restored Porsche and discover later that the word restoration has many meanings, Bruce is the man to set things right. When I asked Bruce to fabricate a fender for a back-to-basics book, he started with a buck, next a fender, and then did part of it twice - as some of my digital images somehow disappeared.

My work often takes me to the shop of Donnie Smith, famous bike builder and long time friend. It was in Donnie's shop that I first met Rob Roehl, back when the shop wasn't much bigger than a two car garage. Since that time, the shop has moved to larger quarters, and Rob has grown into one of the best fabricators in the country.

Creative Metal Works is the small fabrication shop run by Kurt Senescall. It seems like only a few years ago when Kurt went out on his own. In reality, he's been quietly and successfully fabricating cars and parts for nearly twenty years now - more recently with help from Pat Kary.

Another talented fabricator who slaves away in relative obscurity is Neal Letourneau, the man with the testículos grandes to take on a really big fabrication project - building his own Yoder power hammer.

I can only say that even after all these years I still get a rush when the that flat piece of steel turns somehow into a fender or an air clearer. And I'm proud to continue Steve's philosophy and share with thousands of readers what these talented fabricators have shared with me.

Introduction

Over the years we've done a whole raft of sheet metal books. Some are meant for beginning home craftsmen while others are meant for a tin-worker trying to get to the next level. All are useful to anyone with a need or a lust to make their own parts.

Whether your aim is the fabrication of a simple side cover for an old Harley-Davidson FXR, or the creation of a complete fender for some obscure car, you need to stretch and shrink sheet metal. You need to take a flat sheet and give it shape.

So we've cherry picked projects and material from a variety of our books and collected it all here - with the addition of some new material of a more personal nature. Think of this as our Best Hits album, or download to be more current. Everything is here, from Sympathy for the Devil, to All Down the Line, to Wild Horses and Beast of Burden.

And though at Wolfgang we can't claim the body of work, or the financial success, of the Rolling Stones, we like to think we are more than entertainment. We like to think we help people build their dreams. No matter if the dream is attaining the skills of someone like Rob Roehl or Ron Covell, or the dream of finishing that rusty old hot rod in the garage, they're dreams just the same.

Everyone is here: Ron Covell, Steve Davis, Bruce Terry, Craig Naff, Kurt Senescall, Pat Kary, Neal Letourneau, and Mike Pavletic. Collectively that's about 300 years worth of experience and sheet metal wisdom.

So take a perusal through our Best Hits album. Put a real Best Hits album, the re-release of Exile on Main Street, on that beat up CD player in the shop and start pounding on some steel (or aluminum). What you create may not be perfect, but it's yours. And if you persist, the patch panels, fenders and air cleaners you make will only get better and better. Listen to some really early 'Stones and your realize that as good as they were, they still had a lot to learn about playing Rock 'n Roll.

In This Issue

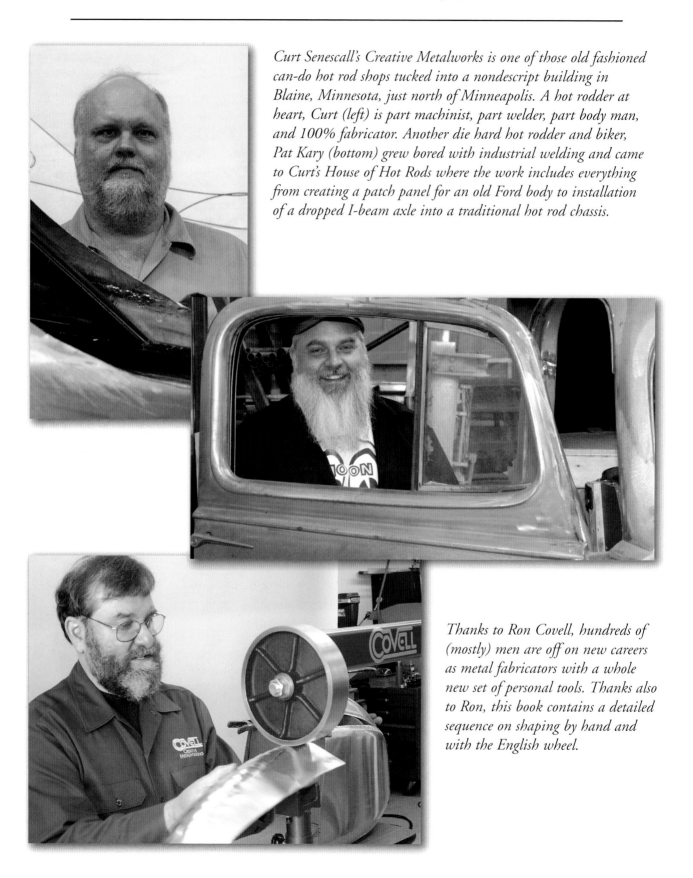

Curt Senescall's Creative Metalworks is one of those old fashioned can-do hot rod shops tucked into a nondescript building in Blaine, Minnesota, just north of Minneapolis. A hot rodder at heart, Curt (left) is part machinist, part welder, part body man, and 100% fabricator. Another die hard hot rodder and biker, Pat Kary (bottom) grew bored with industrial welding and came to Curt's House of Hot Rods where the work includes everything from creating a patch panel for an old Ford body to installation of a dropped I-beam axle into a traditional hot rod chassis.

Thanks to Ron Covell, hundreds of (mostly) men are off on new careers as metal fabricators with a whole new set of personal tools. Thanks also to Ron, this book contains a detailed sequence on shaping by hand and with the English wheel.

In This Issue

An experienced body man, Mike Pavletic (left) got tired of working "for the man," fifteen years ago and moved to a small shop at home. Between then and now, Mike erected a new shop building and made the transition from high-end body work to metal shaping. It's a metal shaping project, the repair of an old AlfaRomeo body, that he's chosen to share with the rest of us.

Rob Roehl spends his time surrounded by choppers and soft-tails. From extending factory Fat Bob tanks Rob has graduated to the fabrication of complete tanks and side panels.

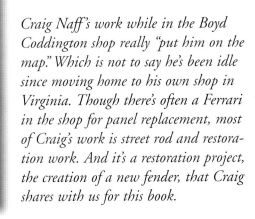

Craig Naff's work while in the Boyd Coddington shop really "put him on the map." Which is not to say he's been idle since moving home to his own shop in Virginia. Though there's often a Ferrari in the shop for panel replacement, most of Craig's work is street rod and restoration work. And it's a restoration project, the creation of a new fender, that Craig shares with us for this book.

Dog Dish

Basic Stretching and Shrinking

Making a "dog dish" is a typical assignment in any beginning sheet metal fabrication class. The project can easily be performed with a minimum of tools, and relies on stretching to create most of the shape. As Rob says, "stretching is what's easiest to do at home."

The first thing Rob does is wipe off the coating of oil. Next comes the first blows from the torpedo hammer. "I like wooden hammers better than plastic," explains Rob. The one "power tool" used here is the small shrinker. As Rob explains, "I find shrinking the edge frames the project, it gives

A simple disc formed into a dish is a very good example of several shaping techniques.

2. I begin with a round face mallet made of hickory. I prefer wood to plastic, but success can be achieved with either. As you can see, I am working the disc into a 12 inch leather bag filled with sand.

it definition so it isn't quite so much like a potato chip from all that tension."

The work with the torpedo hammer and sand bag result in a lot of stretching and walnuts. Rob uses a softer, smaller hammer to work out some of those walnuts. Next comes more shaping with the wooden hammer working over the dolly, and then Rob starts to work just inside the lip, "to try and make that part of the curve more even."

In terms of working with the hammer and dolly, Rob explains that there are really two techniques being used, "When I'm 'on dolly,' hitting the high spots with the hammer and holding the dolly directly under it, it gathers up the area at the peak and it's really half shrink and half stretch. When I'm 'off dolly,' the dolly is not directly under the area I'm hammering, then I'm definitely gathering up the metal."

Near the end Rob uses a slapper instead of a hammer to even out highs and lows. You can see the shiny spots are the highs, the gray areas are the lows. "The hard part is the finishing" says Rob. "I like to really finish the metal, but I'm a minority."

Captions by Rob Roehl

1. We start with a 16 gauge steel disc. I've marked it to roughly show where we will work the two techniques.

3. I prefer to begin in the middle and work to the outside.

4. With just a little effort, mostly in the center, you can see it's picking up shape.

1. Back on the bag for more shaping.

4. After a little more hammering I've stretched a bumpy crown in the disc.

2. Continuing to work from the center to shape the disc.

5. Moving to my post dolly I use a wood slapper with a leather face.

3. Using my hands, I apply pressure to maintain a consistent shape.

6. Here I begin to roll down the edges.

The edges can also be formed with a mallet and a hard surface.

The hand shrinker quickly pulls a lot of shape into the edges.

Continuing the mallet work I choose a wider head. Inset: My favorite wood mallets.

After just a little work we have generated quite a bit of shape.

Now I start to use my hand shrinker to pull down and gather (shrink) the edges.

Then I continue the mallet work to achieve more shape.

Using the mallet against the table I begin to work out some of the lumps.

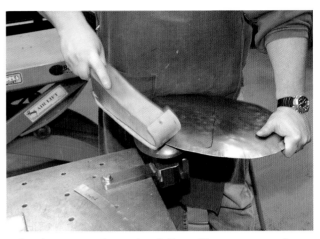

The slapper work on the dolly will continue to shape the edges.

Some hand adjustments.

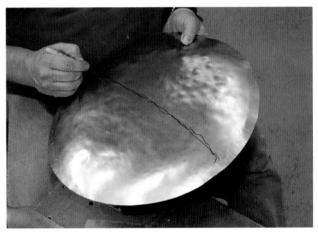

For the sake of time I'll divide the disc and work in quarters.

Again, I work the edges on the post dolly.

I continue to work with the dolly and mallet to begin smoothing out the lumps.

For finish work I will use a metal slap hammer. It has a slight crown.

Continuing the work with the slapper smoothes out the lumps on the disc. The amount of finishing is determined the amount of effort.

Working on the post dolly I'm knocking down the lumps and raising the low spots.

It's easy to see how with a little "elbow grease" the slap hammer has smoothed out the one side considerably.

The slapper is used to even out the edges and pull them down.

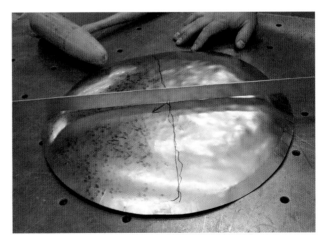

I can continue to work as much crown into it as I desire by pounding in more shape.

Air Cleaner Cover

Another Good First-Time Project

When it comes to building something for your motorcycle that is both aesthetically pleasing and relatively easy to create, an air cleaner cover is near the top of the list. The part is not load bearing, the shape is simple (depending on how crazy you get with the design) and it doesn't affect the operation of the motorcycle. If it falls off or you don't get it done for a month, the bike will still run.

Rob designed this teardrop-shaped air clean-

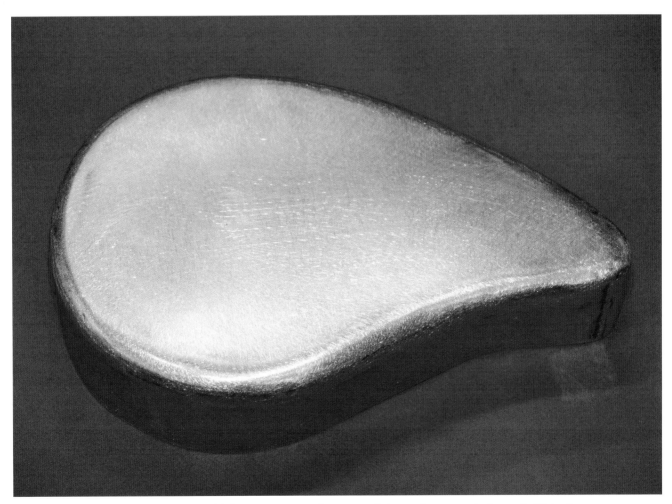

This simple air cleaner cover will add that custom touch to your bike and can easily be embellished to create an even more personal touch.

er cover because, as we just said, "it doesn't have a lot of shape, yet in the end it's a piece you can be very proud of."

THE STEEL

The material is common 16 gauge cold-rolled steel. This is a demonstration project, so for the design Rob just starts out with a common K&N filter element and designs the cover to fit over that element. In the real world you will likely want the cover to fit over the outside of an existing round air cleaner assembly. The cover you make could be held in place on the round air cleaner with two-faced tape or Velcro or whatever fits your needs.

As the pictures show, Rob started by drawing a circle larger than the element and then added the tail. As Rob explains, "I drew out the tail in a shape that I found pleasing." The depth too is determined by the air filter element. Essentially this will be a two-piece part, which helps to keep it all simple.

ADD A LITTLE CROWN

"You could just cut out the flat cover," explains Rob, "and then roll the edge and weld it all together, but that's unacceptable. That would be a pretty crude looking piece." In this case Rob decides to add a little shape to the edge or corner of the air cleaner all the way around. The shape, or crown that he adds at the edge accomplishes two things: It gives the cover a much more pleasing shape, and the crown at the edges gives the sheet metal more strength and minimizes shrinkage and warpage during the welding part of the process.

Rob uses a couple of his favorite T-dollies and body hammers to create a crown all the way around, first the long 2-1/2 inch side-strip, and then the flat part of the cover. "By being patient as I hammer the edges over the dollies I avoid having the main piece (the face of the cover) want to curl. I want it to stay flat, if I did all this work in one or two whacks then it would want to curl."

continued on page 25

A simple sketch on poster board gets me started.

I've left about 1/2" around the air cleaner.

Here I'm measuring the element to find the width of the sides.

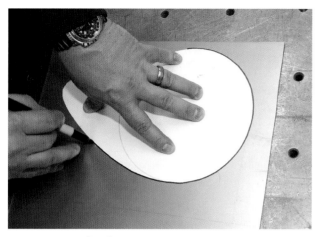

Next, I transfer the pattern to steel and cut it out.

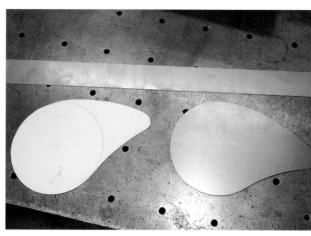

The face plate is cut out of 16 gauge steel.

Now I start a roll on the side of the strip.

Here you see I'm continuing to rock all the way down the strip.

A closer shot of the half roll on the side strip.

Here I change to a big, flat, round post dolly made out of garage junk.

Slowly and patiently I work my way around the face plate...

Beginning to roll the edge of the face panel.

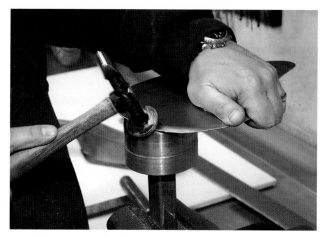

You have to work the edge over gently.

...rolling the edge over the radiused edge of the dolly.

I always try to keep the face as flat as possible.

Rolling over the edge on a reverse curve.

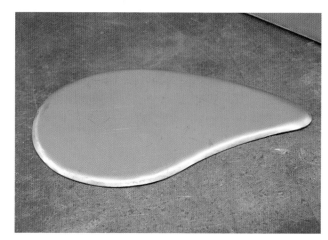

Using a T-Dolly to roll the small end.

The concave section at the bottom of the tail, the area with a reverse curve, is a hard area to shape.

The finished cover with a nice crown all the way around. Note that it's still flat.

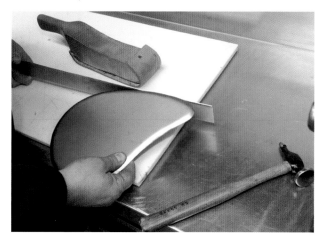

Deciding where to put the seam, I like to start on the tightest corner.

Here I'm rolling side strip on the T-Dolly using a wood slapper.

It starts with one tack weld.

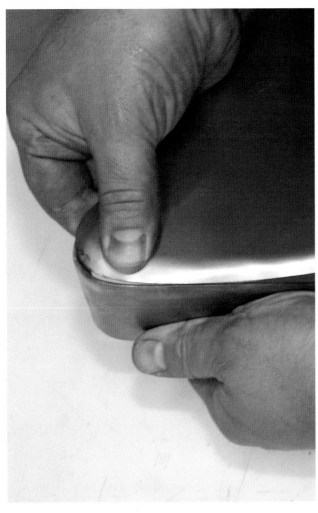

It's important to match the side strip curve to the face plate.

Here you can see we have a good start to our cover.

Then I start to add tacks where the fit is good.

I continue the tack welds while working and holding the side panel in place.

More tack welds are added as the two pieces start to come together.

You can see how I wrap the side piece with my free hand while tacking.

Almost halfway done.

A little tune up on the T-Dolly end to line up the two edges.

I continue to tack my way around. Patience, patience.

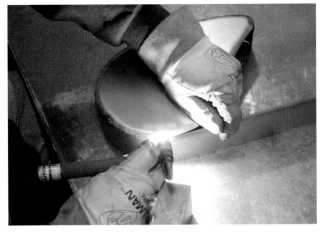

More tacking.

A little more hammer work. Now is the time to fix any bad fitment between the two pieces of metal.

Continue to work and align edges.

More tacking.

A little hand forming.

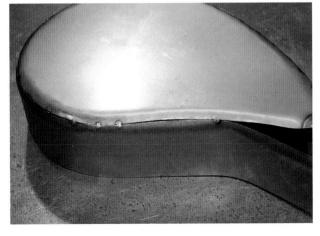

You have to just keep working the edges together.

1. More tacks in the concave area.

3. Working the side panel on a reverse curve.

2. Checking the alignment.

4. Marking the seam for the cut.

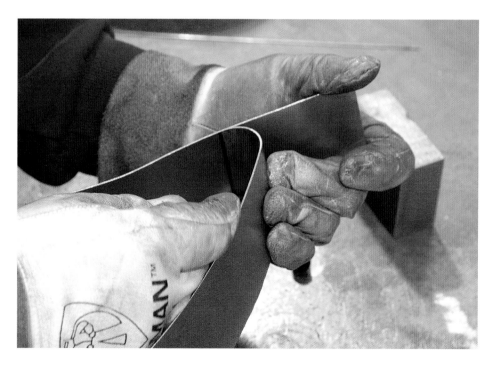

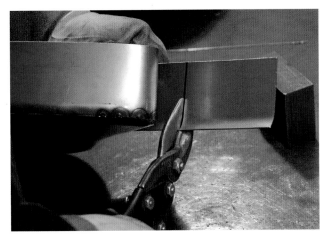

I cut the seam with tin snips...

...and then check the fit.

A little more work on the T-Dolly.

Here I'm tapping the seams down.

Now I can finish tacking the seam.

Here you can see how close together the tack welds are.

Finally the cover is tacked all the way around.

I check the alignment of the seams one last time.

If you have time to weld it - you have time to clean it first.

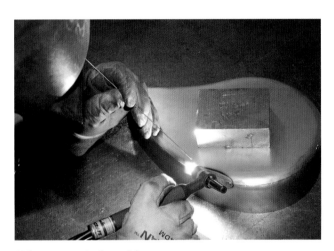

I begin to stitch weld.

Working my way around the cover, filling in as I go.

Here's the finished weld on the cover.

24

If you check the photos you will see that the flat face did in fact stay flat, even after Rob created an edge with a nice radius all the way around the perimeter of the piece. With patience, he was able to do a lot of shaping without having the hammer and dolly work affect the metal - except in the immediate area being worked.

WELDING

The TIG welder is set at 90 amps DC. Again, 90 is the maximum that can be applied, the real amount of amperage is determined by the position of the foot pedal. The first tack weld is a pretty good one because Rob is essentially going to roll this piece to make it match the radius of the cover. Making sure the side strip follows the shape of the cover is a matter of carefully positioning the strip, then keeping it there with a tack weld, then moving ahead and repeating the process. It's often necessary to stop and work the seam with a body hammer, going back to the tack welding. "Working the seam like this, to make sure it's smooth and that the edges are even, saves a lot of time later. This seam will final-weld better, and once it's welded it will require less finish work."

When Rob has the air cleaner cover tack welded together he backs up and starts cleaning the piece before proceeding with the finish welding. "The material must be clean," explains Rob. "You need to get rid of any rust or dirt. Even the oils from your hands will affect the final weld, so be sure you clean the metal of any oils."

"The two pieces of sheet metal fit together so nice you could almost fusion weld them together," says Rob. "I don't worry about total penetration because this is not a load bearing part, I'd rather have a nice seam with minimal warpage."

Finishing the seam starts with a small air-powered grinder, which is used to take the top off the bead, and progresses to an 80 grit pad mounted to a DA. When Rob is done the part is ready for primer, a little more finishing work, and the final paint. It's a unique part that's relatively easy to fabricate and finish. One that's sure to add a nice touch to your motorcycle.

Captions by Rob Roehl

A quick hit on the weld with a small 36 grit disc.

I like to finish parts for paint with my 80 grit disc.

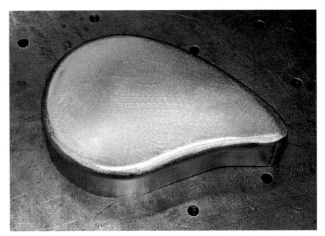

Finished cover ready to be mounted, then off to body work and paint.

Paper Predicts The Project

The following sequence is part of an earlier Harley-Davidson Sheet Metal book. The part being formed is the front corner of a motorcycle gas tank. Of note, the front corner is probably the hardest part of a motorcycle tank to form because it has so much shape. The sequence presented here is an excellent illustration of both the use of a buck, and the way a piece of paper can be used to give a crystal-ball-like look into the future before starting on a particular piece of sheet metal.

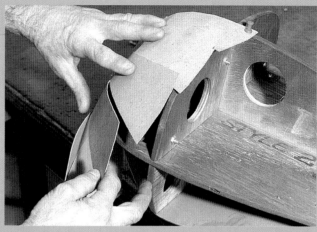

Here he pins the paper to the buck, note the overlap on the various "flaps" of paper.

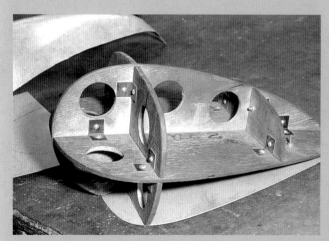

The buck seen here, shaped like the gas tank, is for checking the shape and not for forming. For individuals working at home this could be made from foam.

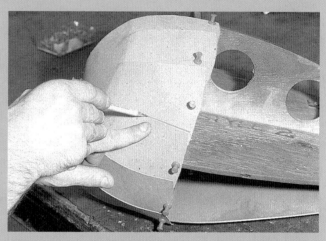

With the paper pinned to the buck, Steve marks the edge of each overlap with a pencil.

Master tin-man Steve Davis cuts long slits in the paper so the slits can overlap and the paper can be "formed" to the buck.

The amount of overlap at each of the joints indicates how much shrinking the metal will have to do there to match the shape of the buck.

Paper Predicts The Project

Steve punches holes that mark the "front" of the tank and transfers those to the metal.

The developing tank section is checked often against the buck. At this point it looks pretty good, though the very front of the tank section needs to be stretched.

The punch holes from the paper are made into a line marked on the metal. This line separates the area that needs shrinking from the area that needs stretching.

With a little ATF as lubricant, Steve uses one of his favorite home-made hammers to stretch the area at the front of the tank.

Steve shrinks the outer area, where the flaps of paper overlapped, with the power hammer.

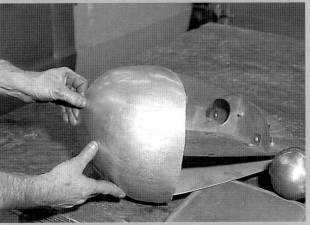

After some finishing work on the planishing hammer, and some filing with a Vixen file, the new tank section is done and ready to weld to the other panels needed to make the entire tank.

Mini Indy Roadster

Half a Half-Midget in Aluminum

In this sequence we follow along as Ron Covell creates the rear body section for a small "half-midget" car. This car is a personal project and not necessarily legal for any particular class of racing. Ron calls it a "half-midget" car because it's bigger than a legal quarter-midget car.

The material being used is aluminum, 3003, H14, .063 inch thick. As Ron explains, "It has a good balance of formability and strength. It's thick enough that you can do some filing and not hurt

Here we see the finished "half midget" car, built from scratch from 3003 aluminum. This is a good project, as each half of the rear body section is made up of three panels (plus the bottom). Fabricating the individual panels forces Ron to use a wide array of tools and techniques, not all of which are the same from one side to the other.

the strength. I've built some race car bodies with .050 but you have to be really careful if you do any filing. Some old Italian race cars were made with .040, but with a race car it's not uncommon for them to end up in the hay bales. And it's really hard to repair those bodies because the metal is so thin to begin with."

"The old Italian cars were crafted from panels that were formed by hand. And yes, they were formed in tree stumps just like we've all heard. Each craftsman would have a hollowed out tree stump and they would just wail away into those stumps until they got the rough shape on a particular panel. I got to tour some of those facilities in the mid-'60s. But that has all changed now. The exotic cars were all hand made in the 1960s, but now those cars are made from pressings or composites."

THE PATTERN

The project starts by making the buck, which is already built in this case. Typically before you can make a buck you need to know what the part is going to look like, you need a good drawing or a blueprint. Ron built this buck pretty much by eye, but he might have used something like the original Kurtis blueprint which he owns (not shown).

As Ron gets down to business he runs a thin metal rod along the area of greatest curvature, explaining as he does, "You want to spread the difficulty between the two pieces instead of making one part really, really hard to make and the other one easy. What you're doing is balancing the difficulty of shaping each piece against the difficulty of welding all those pieces together. For example, a VW body could be made up of a thousand small pieces, each piece would be easy to make but the welding and distortion would be enormous. To take it to the other extreme, making the body from one piece would be ridiculous."

Note: 1/8 inch diameter steel rod is used throughout this sequence instead of welding rod so it will show up better in the photos.

Back to the body at hand. Ron makes a mark on the buck to show where the edge of the metal pieces is going to be. Then he moves the rod to the bottom of the buck and marks that area in the same way. The buck itself is made from medium

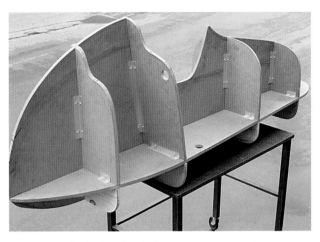

Ron already had a buck for the project, so he can start right in with the layout of the panels.

The location of the seams is marked on the buck. Ron likes to place these in the area of maximum shape.

The patterns are made from light chip board, which Ron positions over the buck.

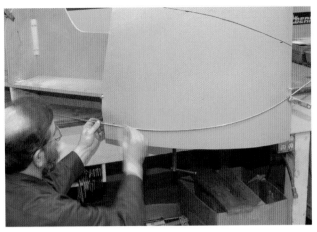

With the help of a steel rod, Ron marks the seam that will separate the side of the car from the bottom.

Much of the cutting is done with a Beverly shear.

With the chip board pinned to the buck, Ron cuts along the marked seams.

The initial shaping is done by hand on the bench...

Then the outline is transferred to a piece of .063 inch aluminum.

...followed by the first of many test fits.

density fiberboard, a material Ron is quick to recommend. "The MDF has a number of advantages over other similar materials. Plywood has rough edges where it's been cut, there may be voids in the material and the density is not uniform. The MDF is uniform and you don't get splinters, and it doesn't kill the edge on your cutting tools like particle board does. I hold the paper on the buck with big push-pins, with MDF the pins can be pushed into the buck instead of being driven in with a hammer. Most commonly I use 1/2 inch, sometimes if you're going to do hammering on it I might go to 3/4 inch fiberboard."

Time now to cut out the pattern, Ron holds the pattern paper onto the form and cuts it a bit oversize. Next he transfers marks on the buck to the pattern paper. This pattern paper is chip board. Then he traces out the curves on the chip board, for both the top and the bottom. Ron doesn't cut right on the line, "I give myself about a quarter inch extra," says Ron.

START THE METAL WORK

Ron marks out the metal using the pattern. It's worth mentioning that you might as well cut out the other side at the same time. An electric shear is used at this stage because it's a fast way to do the first cut, but for the final cut he often uses a Beverly shear or a hand shear.

"To de-burr the edge I use a flat file," says Ron. "I always pull the file toward me and that's for two reasons: First, if you push the file when you're working on sheet metal it will often chatter, but by pulling on the file it hardly ever chatters. And second, when you're pushing the file toward the metal you run the risk of jamming your hand up against the sharp edge if you slip. This way if I slip my hand is moving away from the edge, not toward it."

Next, he puts the gradual over-all shape into the part. This is done before annealing the edges. This initial shaping is done freehand, followed by a test fit. "If I over bend it, I put it on the table and push down on either side The neat thing about this is that it does most of the unbending at the point of contact with the table so you have very good control."

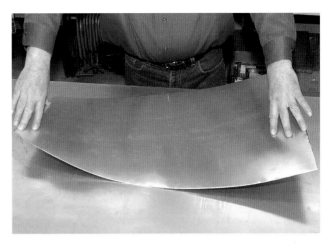

Small adjustments to the curvature of the side panel can be made on the bench.

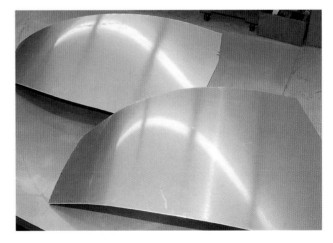

The panel will need more work on the top and bottom, but first Ron gets the basic shape to fit the buck.

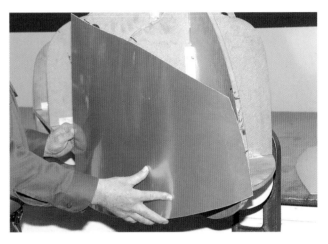

Because the panels are mirror images of each other, it's a good idea to cut and do the initial shaping to both panels before moving on.

Appealing Annealing

Step 1. Adjust the torch to a pure acetylene flame and "dirty" a three inch band along the edges of the aluminum.

Step 2. Re-adjust the torch to a standard blue flame and heat the edge just hot enough to burn off the soot.

Step 3. Repeat step two. The soot burns off at 800 degrees but aluminum melts at 1200 so you have to be careful to keep the torch moving so you don't overheat the metal.

Annealing is the process of bringing the metal back to a dead-soft condition. In the case of this aluminum sheet, it came in a half-hard condition (H14). Ron's goal is to eliminate that hardening before he starts the shaping. Sometimes annealing is used in the middle of a project to eliminate the "work hardening" that occurs as a piece is shaped and shaped and shaped. In any case, it's a useful skill to add to your bag of tricks, so follow along as Ron does this demonstration.

Ron starts the process by bending the panel, explaining as he does, "I curve the parts first because the shape helps eliminate most warpage. If you anneal something that is dead flat it won't be flat when you're finished. Here we need to curl the edges, not the middle, so I'm only going to soften it along the edges."

Ron likes to elevate the part on the bench, simply so he doesn't get the acetylene soot on the table and eliminates the clean up afterwards. Ron puts a layer of soot along a three inch wide band with a pure acetylene flame. The only purpose of the black layer of soot is to act as a temperature indicator. Once he has the piece sufficiently "dirty," Ron adjusts the flame on the torch to a standard neutral flame and heats up the edge of the metal - just enough to burn off the soot. Any remaining soot dusts off fairly easily. Then Ron quenches the piece.

"I quench the pieces when I'm done," says Ron. "This is a non-heat-treatable alloy, so the quenching won't change the properties of the material, but with some alloys you might have to be more careful, they may become brittle."

Now Ron starts to curl the edges down with the shrinker. A process that goes faster and easier than it would have otherwise - if Ron hadn't taken the time to anneal the edge. And that's what it's all about.

"I put the initial shape into the parts first because the shape helps eliminate most warpage that might occur later when the part is annealed. Here we need to curl the edges, not the middle, so I only soften it along the edges."

Ron puts a layer of soot along the edge as described in the side-bar, then adjusts the torch to a more typical blue-white flame and burns off the soot before quenching the piece in water.

Now we need to curl the edges down and the first step in that process is to shrink the edge. The small shrinker shown here is available from Covell and you can interchange the jaws to make it a stretcher as well. The goal is to curve the edges over to match the shape of the buck. "I shrink the edge before I do anything else. What you see is a faceted series of angles on the piece we're shrinking. Once we have the edge positioned where we want it, then we will shape the metal farther in. This is the more efficient way to do it I think."

Ron shrinks across both long edges with the small shrinker. Note how the piece has picked up shape overall from the edge shrinking. Ron flattens it a bit on the table. There's a linkage between the front-to-back shape and the top-to-bottom shape. "So I decreased the curve front to back which increases the curvature top to bottom."

Ron explains that the effects of the shrinking stretch (no pun intended) well beyond the one-inch reach of the jaws. "I've only used one tool and we've created a dramatic amount of shape, much deeper than the one inch reach of the tool's jaws. You don't need tons of tools to create a lot of shape. While we're certainly not done, that one tool has gotten us a long, long way toward the final shape." Note the photos and how the effect of the shrinker reaches as far as three inches in from the edge.

The next step is to check the shape on the buck, "I'm looking at how close the part matches the stations on the buck," says Ron. "We are within about a quarter inch at this point. It has a kind of faceted effect, flat at the edge and then a high crown area. The goal will be to make it a more gradual curve." Note the before picture of the curve at the edge of the metal.

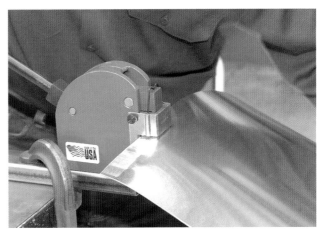

After annealing the two side panels Ron starts shrinking along both edges.

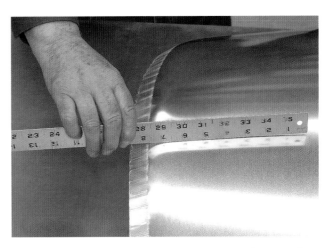

The effect of the shrinking goes well past the actual reach of the jaws and adds crown to the whole piece.

Before doing a test fit, Ron shrinks along the very back edge as well.

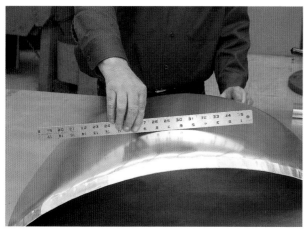

By shrinking the edges, the whole piece has arched up.

Though the edges need a little work, the test fit shows the piece to be quite close.

Here Ron opens up the piece. Though by reducing the crown end-to-end, Ron has actually increased the amount of crown top-to-bottom...

This contour tool can be used to check or document any shape, or to do before-and-after checking of a small area.

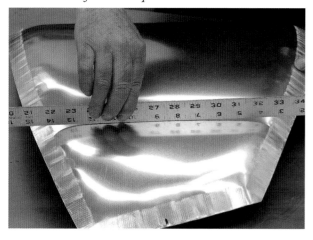

...as is seen here with the ruler.

To create a more rounded edge to the panel, Ron works the area over a dolly mounted in the vise.

To create a more gradual curve Ron starts working the edge of the panel with a slap hammer and a dolly, an old hand dolly welded to a post and mounted in the vise. "I like the slap hammer," explains Ron, "because it covers more area than a regular hammer." It takes time to work along the edges but eventually Ron creates a nice smooth radius all along the edge of the panel.

Once the panel is a fairly good fit on the buck, it's time to punch small holes along the edges. The holes allow Ron to attach the panel to the buck with his heavy duty push-pins. There's still a bit of fine adjusting to do with the slap hammer, working right against the buck. At this point both side panels are shaped and mounted on the buck, with an area of overlap at the back that still needs to be trimmed.

"Now I will establish a centerline for the trimming," explains Ron. This is actually a two-step process. Tape is used first to establish the center line of the outside panel. Then after trimming that panel and re-attaching it to the buck, Ron carefully scribes a line where the "outside" panel meets the inside. Finally the inside panel is removed and carefully trimmed with shears. Once both panels are butted together on the buck it's time to start the tack welding process.

Welding

For welding aluminum like this Ron likes to use 1/16 inch, #1100 rod. The TIG welder is set as follows: alternating current, high frequency control on continuous, medium heat range, flowing 18 CFH of argon. The tungsten used here is a 2% thoriated tungsten, 3/32 inch in diameter. According to Ron, "the books say you should use pure tungsten. But for aluminum sheet metal the 2% holds a sharp tip better and having a sharp tip allows you to focus the weld into a small area which gives you better control." Ron works the seam as he welds, to ensure the two panels stay parallel and in alignment, and that the seam stays close to the buck.

The Dirty Finger Technique

It's time now to make another pattern using what Ron calls the dirty finger technique. "First I tape butcher paper onto the buck with three pieces

Though the effect is somewhat subtle, the contour gauge shows us how Ron has softened the crown at the edge of the panel.

Now the two rear panels can be attached to the buck with pins and tape.

Scribing a cut line where the two panels meet is done by first marking the center line on the outside panel with tape.

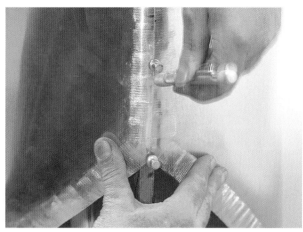

Then the outside panel is removed, trimmed and placed on the buck. Now a line can be scribed on the inside panel where the two will butt together.

Ron does a little fine adjusting of the bottom edge prior to forming a paper pattern.

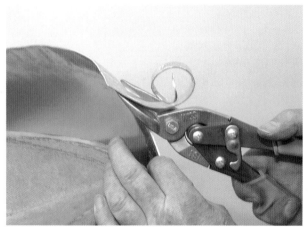

For accurate trimming it's hard to beat good aircraft shears in the hands of a patient craftsman.

The pattern is marked using Ron's famous "dirty finger technique." Fabricators with clean hands need not apply.

With a TIG welder you can get a decent tack weld while the panels are on the buck, with gas it's hard to get any kind of weld because of the wood behind the metal.

After making the paper pattern Ron folds it in half, adjusts the actual outline just slightly and then transfers the outline to the aluminum.

of tape, then I rub my dirty finger along the edge and it leaves a mark that's easy to see."

"I like to fold the pattern in half to judge its symmetry, in this case it's off about 1/2 inch. I will split the difference. That is, I find the line that is half way between the two edges and cut there. Next I draw a centerline on a piece of aluminum and then use the adjusted pattern for both halves."

Now Ron marks the aluminum, trims it first with the electric shear and then does the final trim with the hand-operated Beverly shear. The first step is to create the rough shape, then anneal it as was done before.

Once again, the shrinker is a key part of the shaping process. As Ron explains, "the shrinking is causing the piece to pick up some crown, people don't realize how far in-board the material is shaped even though the shrinker has only a one-inch throat." After the edges are passed through the shrinker it's time for a test fit and then some further adjusting with the hammer and fixed dolly. After another test fit Ron moves to a different dolly with a softer crown, "because I don't want a real sharp curve on the edge of the metal."

Another test fit shows that we need a little more angle all along the edge - which is done with the first dolly and the slap hammer. Now it's rocking on the buck and the point is too far off the buck. "The area where it's hitting the buck is in the center," explains Ron, "so I need to re-contour the metal so it fits the buck better. And by shrinking on either edge, close to the point, it will draw the point down."

The piece needs a little further shaping at the edges, as shown in the photos. Ron spends time working the edges of both the center piece and the two side panels. Then it's time to start scribing lines. The two pieces are taped together and a putty knife is used to keep the bottom under the other pieces. "We are scribing with the bottom panel under the others," says Ron. "You could do it either way but the idea is to keep the seam in the middle of the curve." Ron spaces the tack welds evenly about 3/4 of an inch apart.

After tack welding all along one side, Ron switches and starts the same process on the other

In this case the final cutting is done with the Beverly shears instead of the hand shears. The size of the aluminum panel is slightly larger than the paper pattern.

As before, the initial shape is put into the panel without any fancy tools.

The shape put into the piece in the preceding step helps prevent warpage during this annealing operation.

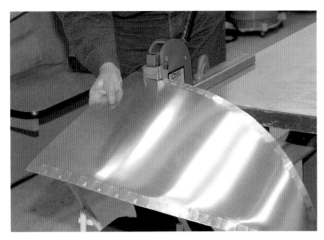

Once the edges are dead-soft, Ron can start shrinking along the perimeter of the bottom panel. Getting enough crown required two sessions on the shrinker.

The first test fit shows that with only a minimal amount of work the bottom panel is very close to its final form.

Nearly any shrinker leaves a shelf or angle at the edge of the area that was in the jaws. Ron minimizes the edge with the slapper and post-dolly.

side. Because this buck is tapered towards the rear, there is no danger that we won't be able to pull the rear section off after it's tacked together.

Tack welding involves a certain amount of tapping and adjusting, for times when one piece slides under the other, or doesn't quite fit. Ron explains that, "The goal for this part of the project is alignment: to make sure the two pieces are flush and to even out the surface. There are places where I drove the metal down to close the gap, but now that they are welded I need to raise those sections by going over the seams with the hammer and dolly."

Fabrication involves a certain amount of planning. Like a good pool player, a fabricator needs to take each shot with an eye toward the next and the next. As Ron explains the strategy, "Before I did anything, I thought about which piece to make first and last. I made the bottom at this stage so I can reach all the seams from the inside."

When the bottom is tack welded all the way around, Ron can go ahead and finish-weld the seam. For this welding Ron uses the same settings as those noted before. "I do it all at once, continuous. If it's two pieces of mild steel with a mild crown I might move around to minimize warpage, but with aluminum and a piece with this much shape, I don't see a problem."

"Sometimes with a piece like this I fusion weld the inside of the seam as well. It looks better and it adds to the strength if there are any places that don't have full penetration. I just go in afterwards and do it with heat, I don't add any filler, I just flow together the metal that's there."

THE THREE PANELS

The three panels are now joined. For sanding the seams Ron uses soap as a lubricant, any bar soap will work. The disc is 50 grit on a standard seven inch grinder. "I have better control with the seven inch," explains Ron. "The goal at this point is to grind off any of the bead that stands up proud above the surface. You of course don't want to get carried away and grind on the metal to the point where you thin the surface."

"If you keep the sanding discs sharp you have pinpoint control as to where it's cutting. Once they get dull you loose that control. People often use the sanding discs longer than they should. "

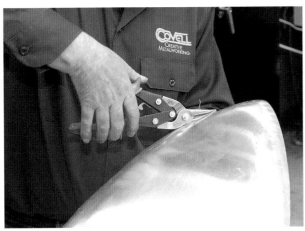

After a little more shrinking and a test fit, Ron can scribe a line where the panels overlap and trim the bottom pan to butt against the two side panels.

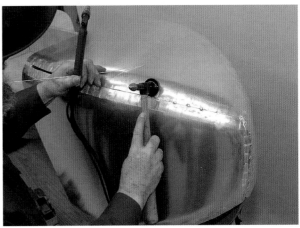

After each tack Ron does a little hammer and dolly work to minimize the gap and keep the two edges even.

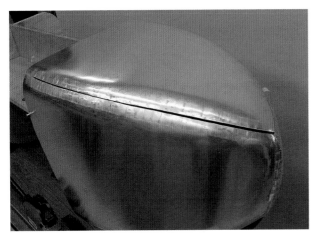

After trimming, the piece is a near perfect fit. Visible gaps can be adjusted slightly as Ron does the tack welding.

Here you can see how Ron holds the bottom panel up tight against the side as he does a tack weld.

Tack welding starts at the point and moves down either side.

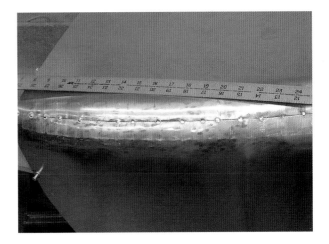

The tack welds are spaced evenly, less than an inch apart. Note the tight gap and the nice way the two edges meet.

Before starting on the final welding Ron works the hammer and dolly along the entire seam.

...so Ron can come back and do the final welding in one continuous pass.

Low spots need to be raised with a small hammer, working from inside, checking the progress after each hammer blow.

Prior to more hand work, Ron runs a grinder over the seam to eliminate most of the additional weld material.

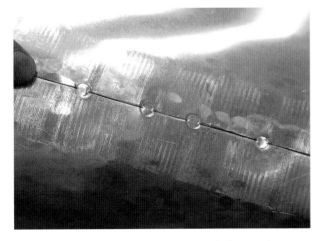

The careful hammer and dolly work leaves the seam in near-perfect alignment...

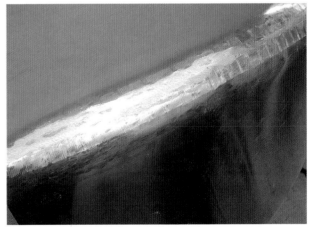

The seven inch grinder and 50 grit disc leave the seam in nice condition, requiring only a bit of finish work to be done later.

Now Ron cuts the weld at the rear of the body so he can pull the two panels together slightly and close up the gap. Ron adjusts the top edge a little so it pulls in tighter against the buck.

PLANNING AND FABRICATION FOR THE UPPER BODY PANELS.

Ron starts planning this section by deciding to make the upper body from four separate pieces of aluminum. "I hold the paper up where it seems to want to lie," says Ron. "That way the paper, and ultimately the metal, won't have to move so very far. Then I lock it in place with the push pins. Once it's positioned, the trick is to push the top down until it meets the center station of the buck. Then I mark it on the far side of the center station (the one running front to rear). That station material is 1/2 inch thick so my line will be 1/4 inch over the front-to-rear center line, making it a little oversize."

Now Ron runs the rod along through the middle (or bottom) of the concave section, the area of maximum shape. He marks that and cuts it out, then cuts out a mirror image for the other side.

Time now to cut out the parts from more of our .063 inch aluminum. After cutting the rough shape Ron trims the parts on the Beverly shear and de-burrs the edge. Both panels are annealed completely, not just at the edges.

The process used to shape these upper panels is much different than that used for the bigger side panels. As Ron explains,"These panels have a lot of shape over every square inch, so I rough shape them with a mallet and sandbag. The first hits are in a line, this is where the metal needs to stretch the most."

Note the change in side to side curvature after the piece is straightened out. Now Ron tries it on the car, it's not a bad fit but we need more of the same. After the second round of mallet and bag work Ron straightens it again, and again we get a huge jump in the amount of side to side curvature. Eventually Ron gets it to the point where it has enough overall shape, though the surface looks like a series of walnuts. Ron switches from a sand bag to a wood block and then to the post dolly and a slap hammer.

Before starting on the upper panels, Ron cuts the rear seam at the top and pulls the two panels tighter together.

The edge of the two side panels must also be adjusted to better meet the new upper panels.

Now it's time to create paper patterns for the upper panels.

After studying the project Ron decides to make the upper panels from two pieces (per side) with a seam along the concave area.

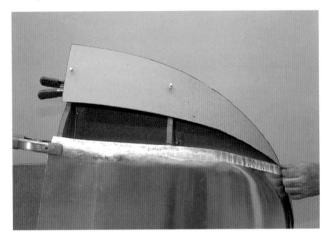

After cutting along the seam Ron has a template of the unshaped upper panel...

...and can go ahead and cut another piece of aluminum.

For the lower part of the panel Ron uses a hammer and a dolly that is much less crowned than the other dolly on the post. Another test fit shows that the panel follows the shape of the buck very well, though we haven't yet started to roll the lower edge. To create the lower roll Ron brings out his secret tool. The edge rolls quite easily against the tube and after only one series of hits the test fit looks pretty good.

Ron does a little more work with the slap hammer against the tube. "The trick," explains Ron, "is to use a found item that has exactly the right radius. You just hit the metal until it bottoms out against the tube, and then it takes on the shape of the tube."

The same shaping procedure is used for the mirror-image panel, though Ron uses the bench-top English wheel to smooth out the surface. Ron uses very little pressure on the wheels, and just moves across the piece the way you would mow a lawn, with very little overlap between one pass and the one next to it. Working with the wheel is fast and the results are smoother than what you get with a hammer and dolly.

Ron does one more series of passes through the wheel, working at a 30 or 40 degree angle to the first. "This is like block sanding," explains Ron. "You change the angle so you make the panel smooth without leaving a pattern." Again, the lower edge is formed against the pipe.

With the two halves of the headrest formed (welding will happen later) Ron cuts another piece of chip board for the middle panel and transfers the measurements to the aluminum. "If you work only with the wheel you might not need to anneal the metal," explains Ron. "The wheel has enough power to move the metal without annealing, but if you work with hand tools then the annealing really helps."

After the center piece is partly formed on the wheel Ron decides to scribe and trim it, and weld it to the top piece. Then finish the forming after it is welded to the left half of the headrest. "There is no point in shaping metal that you are eventually going to trim off," explains Ron.

The initial shaping of the upper piece is done with nothing fancier than a plastic mallet...

To achieve more crown Ron goes back to the mallet and sand bag.

...which causes the panel to curl more than Ron would like.

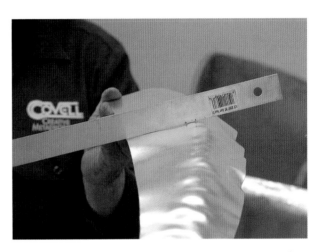

The second round of hammering leaves the panel with a sharp V shape.

After Ron eliminates the curl he's left with the beginnings of a crowned panel.

A test fit shows Ron how far he's come - and how far he still has to go.

At this point the piece has enough shape but needs smoothing, which is done by working against a piece of wood instead of the bag.

Ron does a test fit prior to more finishing work...

...done with a slap hammer and the post dolly.

MORE WELDING

The welding is done off the buck. Ron has witness marks where the two panels line up and will start welding there. It would seem difficult to weld the two panels off the buck and have them fit correctly. But Ron explains that, "They only fit together one way, if you have them the wrong way there's a gap. So it's easy to get them aligned correctly for welding."

The two pieces are joined by tack welds, Ron carefully hammers each one, explaining, "the first thing I'm after as I go through this process is the alignment of the two pieces of metal and the second thing is the contour."

With the two pieces aligned and exhibiting a nice contour Ron goes ahead with the final welding. "I'm trying something new. Instead of welding from the outside of the skin and then fusion welding the inside, I'm going to weld on the inside of the two panels and then fusion weld the outside. It should give us a smaller bead on the outside to clean up."

Ron flattens the bead with the planishing hammer "for speed," and then finishes the hard-to-reach areas with a hammer working over the piece of tubing, explaining, "I could have done the whole thing by hand, but it would have taken a lot longer." The seam is flat and now Ron goes on to the other side.

The only real difference in the creation of the middle panel for the right side is that Ron decided to anneal it prior to shaping, "because the other one was too much of a battle."

Once Ron has the two panels joined to make a complete right side upper section, it's time to weld the two upper body halves together. This nearly-final step in the process starts as Ron attaches the left side upper panels to the buck with stick pins and then runs a centerline with a piece of masking tape. The left side panel is trimmed along the centerline and set back on the buck. Next the right side is set on the buck, with the edge set underneath the left side panel. Now a line is scribed in the right side panel, the panel is removed and trimmed, and the two pieces are tack welded off the buck. Ron does it this way, "so I can get that top seam into the planishing hammer and save

It's a slow process but each test fits shows additional progress.

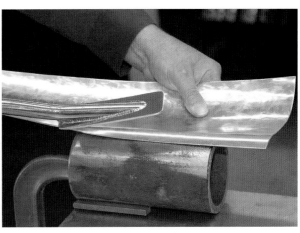

...which is shaped by rolling the aluminum against a homemade fixture with the correct radius.

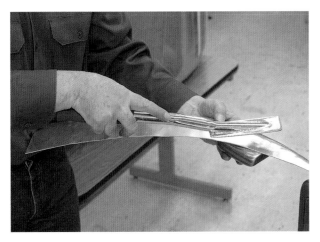

The last of the "walnuts" are eliminated with the slap hammer and dolly.

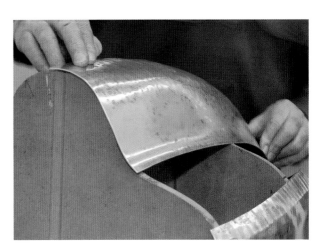

The final check shows a very nice panel - formed completely with hand tools.

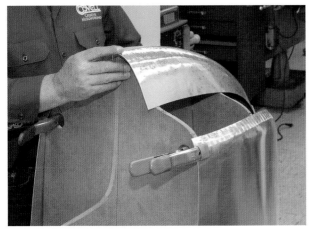

The piece is looking pretty nice, though Ron still needs to begin forming the concave section...

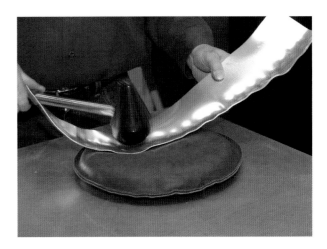

Which means it's time now to start on the upper panel for the right side.

After achieving enough shape by working with mallet and sand bag, Ron decides to smooth the surface with the wheel. "You control how much you raise the metal by adjusting the pressure on the wheels. Here we keep the pressure low."

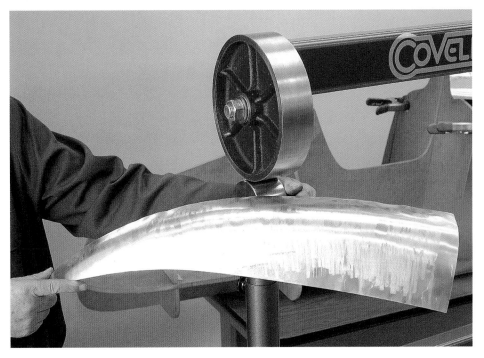

"I'm using an 8-1/2 inch radius lower wheel, a radius that matches the shape of the part. By rolling the short way I'm able to use a low-crown wheel."

myself a bunch of time." By tack welding off the buck Ron is able to move the two pieces around to keep the joint nice and tight at the point of each tack weld. Once the seam is tack welded and massaged over a dolly the final welding can begin. This is done conventionally with the bead on the outside and a fusion weld along the inside.

The top section is now welded into one unit. Ron finished the top seam in two ways. Closer to the front he used the English wheel which did a great job of flattening the seam. "I did this without grinding the bead first, so that extra metal has to go someplace. In this situation it raised the top of the headrest slightly, which is OK because the fit against the buck was a little tight to begin with. Normally, I would probably grind the bead first, then run it through the wheel."

For the tail-end of the body section Ron knocked the bead down with a sander in a more conventional fashion, followed with a few passes through the planishing hammer.

Ron attaches the new top section to the buck with two dry-wall screws. Once attached to the buck he scribes a line, pulls the section off the buck and trims the lower section using hand shears. After trimming Ron screws the top section back onto the buck then does a little final adjusting of the metal

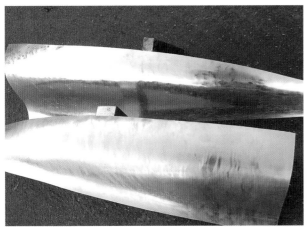

The two finished panels. Note the difference in finish between the piece that was wheeled (lower) and the one finished with hammer and dolly (upper).

As Ron continues to work the metal he changes the angle of attack to avoid leaving any pattern in the metal.

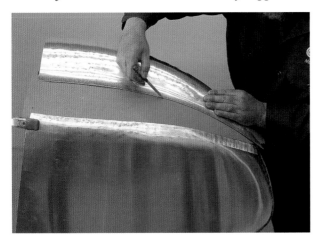

With the upper panel clamped in place Ron marks out a pattern for the center panel.

Ron is using a higher-crown lower wheel here that allows him to wheel along the length of the panel.

The center panel is shaped entirely on the wheel, without any annealing first.

Ron starts the tack welding at one end, and closes up the gap as he moves up the seam.

Note how the two pieces come together as Ron tack welds his way up the seam.

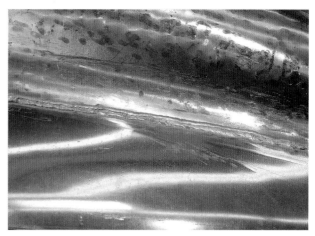

To minimize the size of the bead, Ron welded the bead on the inside of the two panels, then "flowed" the seam on the outside.

Before doing the final welding, Ron puts the piece on the buck and checks the fit...

Before finishing the seam Ron knocks down the bead, which is on the inside this time.

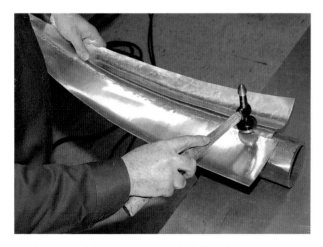

...then carefully hammer and dollys the entire seam.

The planishing hammer speeds up the finish work.

at the edges. Now the tack welding can commence. Ron starts at the tail end with two or three tack welds, and then starts up one side and then the other. After each tack Ron adjusts the metal at the site of the tack weld and also just "downstream," Sometimes a small cut-off putty knife is used to bring the two parts back to a butted condition if one edge slips under the other. Following the tack welding it's time to peel the part off the buck, hammer and dolly both seams, and then do the finish welding.

METAL FINISHING

As Ron explains, "The traditional method is to hammer every square inch of the bead until they are perfectly smooth both inside and out. Whether or not you actually finish it to that level is up to you."

The first step is to knock down the bead with the electric sander, followed by a Vixen file and some careful hammer and dolly work all along the seam. This is a process that's easier to explain through a series of photographs, and that's what we've tried to do here, starting with the proverbial "before" picture and ending with a perfectly smooth seam.

INTERVIEW, RON COVELL

Ron, can we talk a little about bucks, the different kinds of bucks and the advantages and uses of each?

There are many types of bucks. The wire type is one of my favorites. Typically they are made from steel round rod, 1/8, 3/16 or 1/4 inch diameter. What I like is, they are fast to construct, well suited to long sweeping curves and real easy to change. With wood, if you need to shave off some material that's easy, but it's cumbersome to add material. With wire, you can cut one element loose, re-contour it and re-attach it.

The bucks that most of us are familiar with are made from MDF (medium density fiberboard). The advantage to these types of bucks is that they're relatively cheap, fast to make and you can pick up as much detail as you need. The number of stations can change per the contour. That is, you use more stations where there is more shape.

Trimming and fitting the two upper halves starts as Ron marks the centerline on the left half. The process is the same as that used for the two lower side panels.

Again, tack welding starts at one end and moves along...

...with adjusting and occasional hammer and dolly work between the individual tacks.

49

Here you can see Ron positioning one panel so it's tight up against the other while doing another fusion weld.

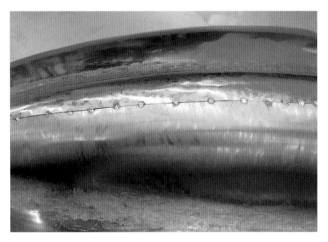

The welds are placed evenly all along the seam.

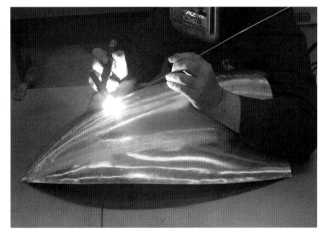

Once Ron is happy with the way the two panels fit together, he can go ahead and do the finish weld in one continuous seam.

Portions of the buck can be made very rugged, so they can be hammered on.

Some people use clay, this is expensive, but picks up fine detail which makes it easier to envision the overall shape. No gaps to visualize. You can read the shapes with the highest degree of accuracy.

Foam is faster, I've seen people use insulation foam from builder supply companies. That's OK, but it doesn't sand or shape as easy as surfboard or urethane foams. These come in a wide range, from light to dense, and can be shaped with great precision.

And there's paper mache', you can make a form quickly from chicken wire and strips of newspaper dipped in glue. You have a nice form at very low cost. A buck is generally too flimsy to hammer on. A buck is most often used as a template.

What are the skills an individual needs to develop in order to begin making more advanced shapes?

Let's just say the people with persistence pick it up. The best indicator of success is persistence, it doesn't come easy for most people. Good hand-eye coordination is paramount. In addition, I would encourage them to learn welding very early in the process. It's so essential to almost anything you do. A lot of people struggle with the welding part.

So do people need a TIG, or heli-arc welder, to do big sheet metal projects or is a gas outfit good enough?

Starting out with gas is what I would recommend, in time I would encourage them to get a TIG welder….. because it gives you more control. Control of heat and puddle size is a real advantage. With the TIG you can make a tiny weld that's easy to finish and work, it gives you good workability of the weld area.

Advanced sheet metal means bigger more complex shapes. Can you talk about the seams? How does a person decide where to put the seams, and how does he or she decide how many pieces to use in creating an individual part?

Beginning metal shapers usually make things from more pieces because their skill in shaping is moderate and they would rather have the seams to deal with. As they develop more skill they often use fewer and fewer pieces. Once you have control

A small lower wheel is useful for working a tight radius. Here Ron shows how the wheel from his benchtop unit can be adapted to the full-size wheel.

The top seam also blends neatly into the panel on either side after a few passes through the wheel.

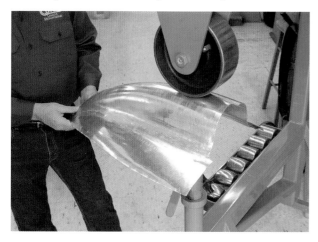

For this finishing operation Ron wants the lower wheel's radius to match that of the headrest.

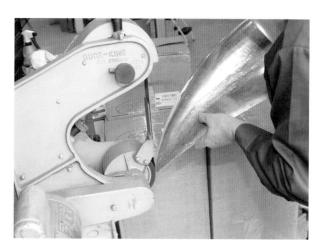

To finish the lower part of the seam, Ron first grinds off the excess material...

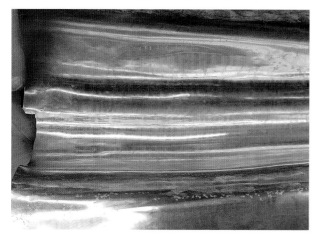

The combination of a fusion weld on the inside followed by the passes through the wheel, leave the inside of the bead nearly invisible.

...and then passes the seam through the planishing hammer.

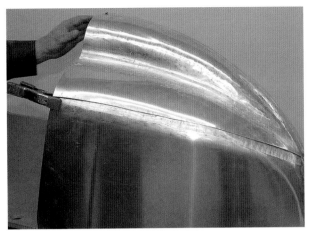

Now it's time to clamp the upper assembly to the lower.

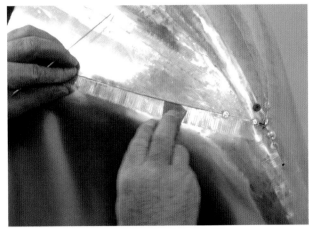

After screwing the upper section back on the buck, Ron aligns the two panels...

Then scribe a line where the two panels overlap.

...and starts the tack welding sequence.

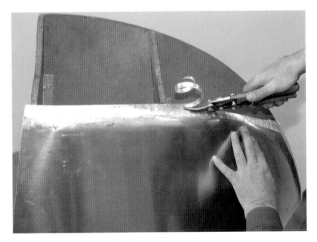

Then trim the lower panel to create a nice butt-joint.

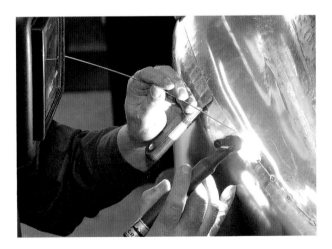

Occasionally Ron has to hold the putty knife in place while he does the nearby tack weld. In this careful fashion he works his way up the seam.

you can make the pieces bigger and it speeds up the fabricating process. There's another benefit of fewer pieces: if you're making a '40 Ford rear fender and you make it from 6 pieces it's hard to keep the continuity of shape, or flow, after all the pieces are joined. The tools you work with make a difference too. By hand it's hard to make big pieces, but if you have a wheel or a planishing hammer then it's much easier to make larger pieces.

The overriding idea is to make the part from the smallest number of pieces that you can; consistent with your ability to shape metal. A smaller number of pieces means less warpage from welding and less weld clean up.

How should people decide where to put the seams?

You can shrink, stretch or bend a piece of metal. Every part must be made using combinations of those. Since I don't have power shrinking equipment, I can only shrink a limited amount; I can only work close to the edge. So most of the shaping I do is done by stretching - because of this it makes the most sense to put seams in the middle of the areas of greatest curvature.

The equipment you use has a lot to do with it. With a Pullmax that can shrink 36 inches into a panel, you can do things that I simply can't, and it affects the initial layout of the part.

What kind of tools are needed for advanced sheet metal work?

I would say get a TIG welder first. Next, a more sophisticated shrinking machine, to go past the limits of the one that I have, it gives you a lot more capability. Next some sophisticated way to stretch and smooth large pieces, a wheel or hammer of some kind.

What holds people back from bigger more complex projects?

People are be afraid to make mistakes. No one's gone far in this business by doing things the same way over and over. Don't be afraid to try some new things - at the risk of throwing away a few panels.

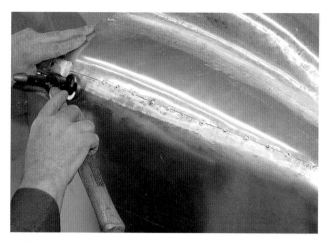

Following the tack welding Ron starts to hammer and dolly the seam.

The small grinder can be employed anywhere there's a blob of metal on the inside of a tack weld, this eases the hammer and dolly work.

With the inside lumps out of the way, it's time to finish the hammer and dolly work. The radius of the dolly is close to the inside radius of the seam area.

We've decided to end the chapter with a finishing sequence. Thus the "before" picture of the seam after one pass with the electric grinder.

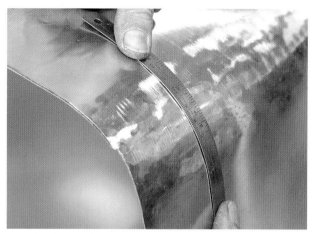

... which results in quite an improvement in the surface contour.

Another perspective on the before condition of this seam.

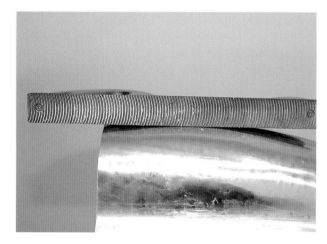

A sharp vixen file is used here for at least two reasons.

First, Ron knocks down the obvious high spots and raises the low areas...

As Ron files across the seam he will knock down the highs, and thereby identify the lows.

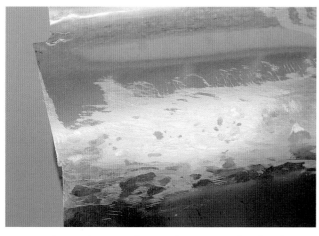

...as is shown here at this mid-point in the finishing sequence.

Note the elimination of nearly all the low spots.

Ron uses one of his own picks to raise the low areas...

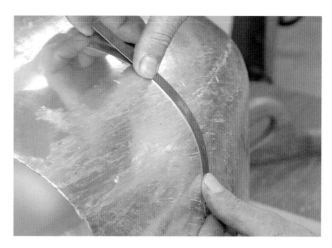

A fact that's confirmed by this side view. How far you go with the finishing, "is really up to the fabricator."

...followed by a bit more filing. Ron is careful so the amount of material he removes with the file is minimal.

Here we have the finished body seam on a complete rear body section.

Welding Steel

Gas & TIG for Sheet Metal

To get a handle on the requirements for sheet metal welding, along with a short Welding 101 class, and a discussion of the pros and cons of steel and aluminum, we stopped in at Creative Metalworks in Blaine, Minnesota. While owner Kurt Senescall answered my questions, employee Pat Kary did a variety of welding demonstrations.

The demonstrations include TIG (or heli-arc) and gas welding applied to both sheet steel and

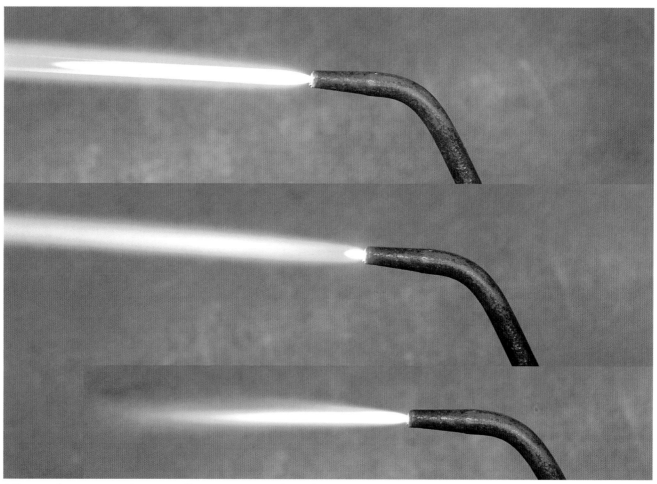

The top flame is a carburizing flame, more acetylene than oxygen. The 2nd flame is a neutral flame, notice the large soft flame cone is gone. This is the flame used for most welding procedures. The 3rd flame down is an oxidizing flame. The easiest way to tell an oxidizing flame from the others is the hissing sound you will hear when too much oxygen is introduced.

aluminum. Pat also did a short demonstration of silicon-bronze "welding" of steel. We left gas-welding of aluminum out of this series as Ron Covell did such a great job illustrating those techniques in Chapter Eleven.

Today, most shops do their sheet metal welding of either steel, or aluminum, with the TIG welder. Yet, even an inexpensive or used TIG is about a thousand dollars. So part of the idea here is to illustrate the fact that while the heli-arc might be nice, you can indeed weld sheet metal with an old-fashioned oxy-acetylene welder.

Q&A, KURT SENESCALL

Kurt, What are the pros and cons of using steel for sheet metal fabrication?

Steel lasts longer, it's cheaper, and for a lot of people it's easier to weld. But on the other hand, it's harder to form. Some steels, like the aluminum or silicon-killed steel sheets, are easier to form, but cost more. These are drawing quality steels, created by adding a little aluminum or silicon at the end of the steel-making process. The net result is a steel sheet that's easier to form, but I don't think you really need these unless you're making really extreme shapes or using a die set.

What are the main pros and cons of using aluminum for sheet metal fabrication?

Kurt Senescall decided to open his own shop nearly 20 years ago and he's still in that same building in Blaine, Minnesota, today. This dragster is a recreation of the Tom Hoover top fueler from the late 60's. The original was built by Woody Gilmore and bodied by Tom Hanna. The body is formed from .060 3003 H14 aluminum and welded with 1100 rod. Learn more at http://cacklefest.com/Hoover.shtml.

Here Pat has tack welded one end of our demonstration piece.

1. Then he tack welds the other end. It will take a few seconds for the metal to melt and a puddle to form. The size, and the angle, of the torch tip will put more or less heat on the panel.

2. Form the puddle, add rod, move.

3. One more time, form the puddle, add rod, move...

4. Hammer and dolly work on a gas weld is easiest to do when the metal is still hot. Again, only hammer and dolly as much as needed to relax the metal.

5. The process continues.

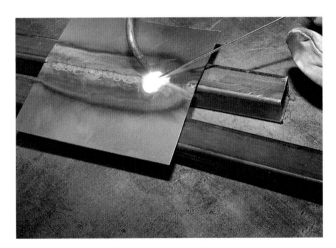

6. Notice the tacked end. Tack the panel every 4 inches or so, and then tack equal spaces between those tacks, before starting the solid weld.

3. *Notice that Pat is working the weld. Since the weld caused the distortion it is the place to work to relieve it.*

Aluminum is easy to form and can be polished, but it's harder for some people to weld. Typically you are using thicker material than you would with steel, so you have more material to work with when you get to the sanding and filing stage. Aluminum is measured in decimals, the .060 inch material is a common thickness for fabrication projects. You can go thicker though and still have good workability.

In the end it's the product and how it will be used that determines whether you use steel or aluminum. Aluminum bike tanks are easy to form but they tend to crack, so again it's the application that's important.

If I don't generally need the A-K steel for fabrication, what grade of steel do I want?

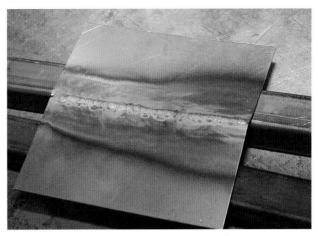

1. *The finished weld, still hot from the torch.*

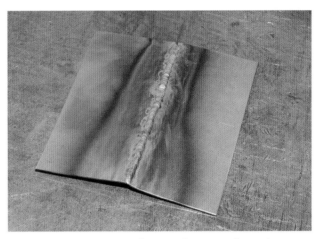

2. *This is a pretty small piece, but note how the shrinkage caused the seam to rise up.*

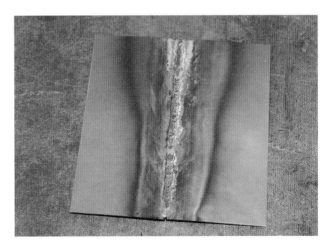

4. *With a little work on the bead with the hammer and dolly, the bead is stretched slightly and the weld is relieved. The result is a flat piece of steel.*

59

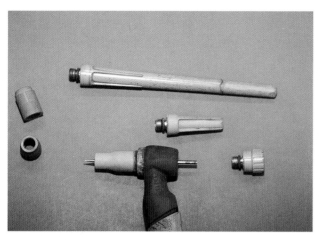

The torch can be made to fit smaller areas by using a shorter ceramic cup, or a shorter end cap.

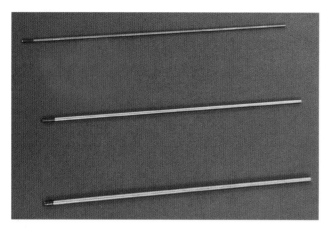

Tungstens come in various thicknesses. 3/32 inch is the most versatile. The 1/16 inch is used for welding very thin materials.

The point should be sharp. I use a longer taper than this for welding sheet material. The longer and sharper the point the more precise the welding can be.

Again, tack every 4 inches or so, and then go back and tack between those tacks.

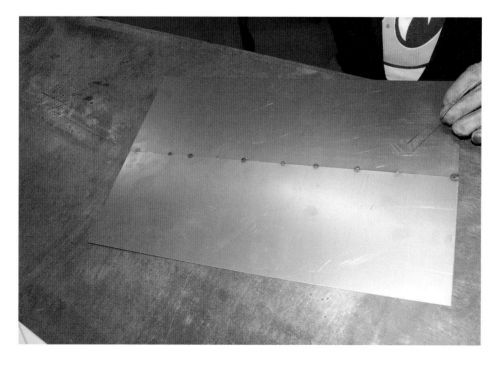

You want cold-rolled mild steel, the 1018 alloy in 18 gauge is ideal for most projects, 19 gauge is nice if you can find it. You do not want hot rolled, it's dirty and has a scale on the outside, which you have to clean off before you can start fabricating. I always buy my steel from a good supplier and tell them I want steel made in the US of A. Some of the sheet metal from overseas is brittle and will crack when you bend it.

Kurt: What are some of the types of aluminum sheet commonly available?

The most available are, 1100 H14, 3003 H14, and 5052. The 1100 is pure aluminum, so you can form it easily. In terms of strength, the 1100 is the weakest. Also, it does not work harden, while the others do. Sheets of 3003 are the most common, this alloy would be good for any kind of body panels, or something like a gas tank. If necessary, you can anneal the whole sheet or just one spot.

What about the hardness designation, the "H-14"?

The hardness designation differs depending on the alloy. For the 3003, H-14 is considered half-hard. Zero would be dead soft. I explain to people that the hardness is a property of the material, while tempering is something that was done to the material after manufacture. For this type of work it's good to avoid tempered material.

What are the advantages of using the TIG or heli-arc for welding in place of a gas welding outfit?

With TIG welding, everything is cleaner and stronger. The heat-affected-zone is smaller, and as a result you tend to get less shrinkage of the sheets. There is a big difference between TIG and gas for welding aluminum - the TIG is a much nicer weld.

Let's talk about the tungsten you use for the TIG, and do you always use a sharp point on the tungsten?

You can buy pure tungsten. I like 2% thoriated, it's radioactive and you can tell these from the others by the red ring around the end. This

With the tungsten about 1/16 to an 1/8 inch away from the panel, start the arc, add pedal (heat) until you form a puddle then add rod, move, form puddle, repeat.

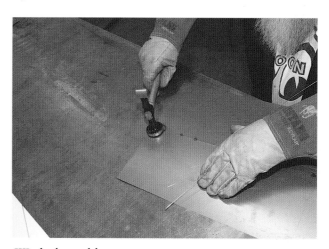

Work the weld area as you go.

Weld in about one inch or shorter increments. Hammer and dolly. Repeat..

Shopping for a TIG at MWS

For more information on welders, and TIG units in particular, we spent an afternoon at the Mississippi Welders Supply Co. store. The company has 8 stores, we spent our time with Troy Elmer in the Hudson, Wisconsin location. During the Q&A with Troy, he pointed out the best values in welding equipment and some of the features to be found on the newest TIGs.

Troy, are TIG welders getting more and more common, especially among home users?

Yes, especially in the last 5 years. There are more reasonably priced models on the market now than there ever have been.

Can you describe the machines that a person at home, or in a small shop, might consider buying?

A basic DC (direct current) TIG welder starts at $900.00. This is what I call a thin-gauge machine, it doesn't have enough power to weld heavy material. You are limited to 12 or 14 gauge steel or stainless, no aluminum.

For about $2,000.00 you get a full feature TIG machine. This machine will have DC and AC, that way you have can use the AC for aluminum. For the extra money you get the AC, and you get higher amperage to weld heavier material. Another thing is the pulsing, this unit will have pulsing built in. And more money gets you a higher duty cycle as well.

We also have one machine at fourteen to fifteen hundred dollars that does have AC and DC, but no pulsing.

What's the advantage of pulsing?

Pulsing reduces the heat input, which is good for thinner materials, and it gives you a better-looking bead.

When you send a person out the door with the new welder, what do you recommend for a tungsten and rod, assuming they are going to weld sheet metal?

I recommend the 2% thoriated tungsten. In terms of rods, the 70s works well for regular steel.

Do you offer classes for people who buy a welder?

No, but all the local technical colleges do. They have really good night classes that cover all phases of welding.

Where do people make mistakes with a new TIG machine? And are there issues involved with the new welder that people didn't think about ahead of time.

For mistakes, sometimes they get the polarity wrong, or they use the wrong gas. A MIG welder uses a mixed gas, a TIG should use only straight argon.

At Mississippi Welders Supply they stock a variety of welders, from relatively inexpensive MIG and TIG units to full-blown commercial units meant for a busy commercial shop.

Shopping for a TIG at MWS

The other hidden issue is the amount of power you need to run it. Most of the machines, especially the older ones, use a transformer and they require a pretty heavy circuit. Our midrange fifteen hundred dollar machine needs a 50 amp 220 outlet and the two thousand dollar machine needs 55 amps.

There are some machines that use an inverter instead of a transformer and these don't need such a heavy circuit, and they're lighter machines as well. A machine with an inverter and the same capacity as our midrange machine only needs a 20 amp 220 volt circuit. Some of these will run on more than one voltage source, like 220 single or multi-phase, even 110 volt, but only if you have a 28 amp 110 circuit. The inverter machines do cost more, two hundred to a thousand dollars more than a similar transformer-equipped machine.

You don't have to buy a TIG. A small setup like that shown above fits easily on a shelf in a small shop and can be used to weld both steel and aluminum.

How do you feel about the various brands of welders?

We sell Miller so obviously we like the Miller brand. I tell people to buy one of the big three; Miller, Lincoln, or Thermal Arc, because all are made in the US, you get better service and warranty, and if there are any problems it's easier to get parts or service later.

What about gas-welding outfits, how much less are they?

Quite a bit. The small setup we have on the counter with the small tanks is two hundred and ninety five dollars. And If you buy the Smith Tuff Cut, it's about five hundred dollars including the standard tanks and a cart.

The Econotig from Miller is a good welder for a small shop and offers both AC and DC operation and an output of 150 amps.

Hammer and dolly as needed after each weld. Doing this while the panel is still hot is easier, but it can be worked cold…

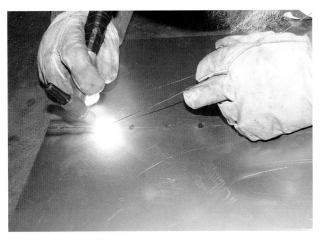

…another bead in process.

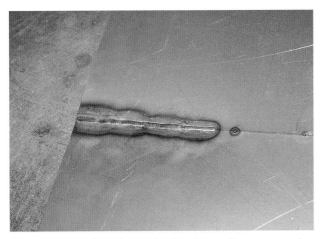

This progress shot shows the bead run from one tack weld to another.

Two demonstrations, one gas welded (upper) one TIG welded (lower). Notice the smaller heat-affected-zone in the TIG-welded example.

is a pretty universal tungsten. Rare earth tungstens are very good for welding aluminum if you can find them.

I always sharpen it to a long tapered point, some say "ball" the end, but the point does burn back by itself if it needs to. It is easier to control the weld when you have a point, even on sheet aluminum.

What rods are available and commonly used to weld aluminum, and does the alloy of the rod need to match the alloy of the sheet?

Typical aluminum rods include 1100, 4043, and 5356, and these come in typical sizes. The 1100 is pure aluminum, so it's the most ductile. This is good if you need to hammer on the bead, or flatten the bead, but the seam is not as strong.

The 4043 is useful for lower grades of aluminum, like castings for example. This would be

Pat Kary spent many years doing production welding and much prefers the relative freedom of fabricating and welding street rod and motorcycle parts.

good if you are welding a Harley head.

The 5356 is a higher grade aluminum rod. This is good for sheet plate, and welding good grade aluminum and billet aluminum. The 5356 provides the best color match for anodizing, if that's a consideration. Don't use base metal as rod. Welding rod is meant to be rod, the alloys in the base metal are not meant for welding.

What about the rods used for heli-arc welding on steel?

There are two basic steel rods, one is oxy-weld65, the other is ER70s, they are very similar, but come from different manufacturers. The number indicates the tensile strength. For example, an 80s D2 is a good rod for chrome moly, and has a high tensile strength. For mild steel though, I use the oxy-weld65 or ER70s.

You can also use silicon bronze rod. The advantage is the low temperature; you don't melt

...weld again...

...and hammer again.

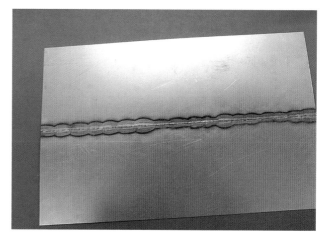

The end result is a nice, neat bead that's strong, yet exhibits very little warpage.

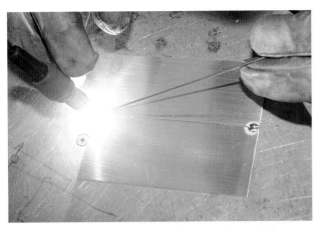

1. *Aluminum may take a bit more to heat before a puddle forms because it dissipates heat so rapidly. Use Scotch brite or clean all areas to be welded including the welding rod before you start!*

2. *Again, as with steel, tack about every 4 inches, then tack between the tacks before welding.*

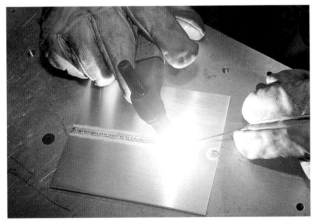

3. *Unlike steel, with aluminum it is actually easier to hammer the weld flat after the welding process has been completed.*

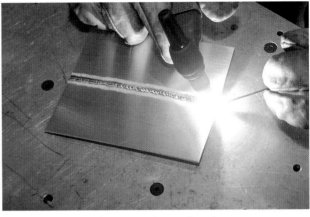

4. *If you touch the tungsten to the aluminum or touch the rod to the tungsten you must resharpen the tungsten. Otherwise you will contaminate the weld, and have a harder time controlling the arc.*

5. *The top side of the finished weld, the next photo shows the back side - aluminum welds may not penetrate all the way through.*

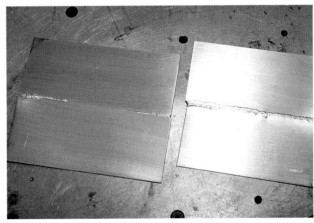

6. *Penetration is important - if you plan to metal finish or hammer the weld flat you should weld the back side also or it will crack. Use Scotch-Brite or clean the back side of the seam before welding.*

the base metal as you weld. You can't use this material for butt welds, but only when the metal overlaps or you are doing a T-weld. The silicon bronze almost sweats in like soldering. This would be good for any joint that needs to withstand vibration. A silicon bronze weld will hold body work well, and also holds chrome. It's available in all the standard sizes, starting with .030 inch, then 1/16 inch and all the rest.

With silicon bronze there is no flux, so there's no contamination to affect any process that comes later. This is good for header flanges or a tube goes over another tube with a snug fit.

Is there a general rule of thumb for choosing the size of the rod?

As a loose rule of thumb, the rod should match the thickness of the material being welded. Also, the width of the bead should be twice the material thickness.

Where do people make mistakes when they weld sheet metal?

They forget to use quality materials and they are not careful enough about cleanliness. You can't have any paint, rust or Bondo on the metal. And always buy good steel from a good yard, never use hot rolled steel.

Captions by Kurt Senescall

A finished silicon bronze weld. Note that the weld looks like bronze and does not look burnt. Overheating will cause the weld to turn black or charcoal-looking. These silicon bronze welds are very durable and strong, and withstand vibration and flexing well.

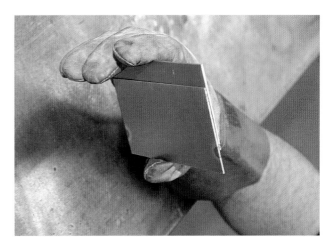

Silicon bronze is an excellent and easy rod to work with. Never use for a butt joint though.

Low heat is used. Use just enough heat to let the rod melt to the base metal.

Chapter Five

Hammer History

From Plowshares (and Swords) to Body Panels

Power hammers are such an essential part of metal forming, and of this book, that it seemed only logical to spend a little time talking about how they originated and where the modern craftsman might find a power hammer to buy, or at least parts for some of the old standards.

AN ABBREVIATED HISTORY OF POWER HAMMERS

The two names that come up most often when people speak of serious power hammers are

The real McCoy, a double-ended Yoder. Working with a power hammer with two ends, a hard-working metal shaper can put shrinking dies on one and stretching dies on the other, or two slightly different stretching dies on either end.

Pettingell and Yoder, which is not to say that either one of these machines was the first or the most successful power hammer on the market.

The first power hammers were used for forming and forging, seldom for what we call shaping. As early as the sixteenth century (and probably earlier) mechanized hammers were used for drawing out shapes in iron. The earliest hammers were simple "helve" designs, really nothing more than a hammer head on the end of a lever. The arm was raised and then released by a simple mechanical linkage. As the mechanical revolution progressed, more efficient crank-operated, vertically oriented hammers came to market. By applying the power and speed of a power hammer to a set of closed dies, forgings could be manufactured on an economical basis.

Power hammers tend to be made from huge, heavy cast parts. Without all that mass, there's no way the structure could withstand the incessant pounding and inherent vibrations. Early advancements in power hammers involved not just speed or size, but a means of isolating the hammer and drive mechanism from the vibrations. Atmospheric and pneumatic hammers

Part of the Yoder's beauty is the ease with which the length of the stroke can be adjusted.

attempted to isolate the structure from the blows of the ram by attaching the ram to a piston contained in a cylinder. The simplest atmospheric hammer lifted the ram and piston, which created a vacuum under the piston. When the ram was released or tripped, the vacuum added force to the descending piston and ram, which was no longer connected directly to the structure of the machine.

Die support mechanism on a Yoder bears a remarkable resemblance to the assembly first patented by Mr. Shaw in 1866. The spring and strapping arrangement helps to isolate the frame from bad vibes and allows for a dead blow.

How to Build a "Yoder"

Q & A WITH NEAL LETOURNEAU

Neal, tell us first why and how you decided to build a Yoder?

It's all about work, it does more work than you can do alone. More work in less time.

Why not just buy one?

They're hard to find and phenomenally expensive. Plus, if I build one I can update the drive system for more efficiency and less maintenance.

Where did you start on this quest?

I called Yoder, got Bill Hacker on the phone, and he told me about Clay Cook and Jim Hervatin (see Sources). Jim built his own Yoder so I called him and asked him some questions. He let me drive down and dimension his machine, he got me started. I bought the bottom tool post, connecting rod, spring mount and the clutch from Jim. Everything else I came up with on my own.

Do they still make Yoder hammers?

They've only made one hammer in the last 20 years, and that was for a Korean aircraft company. Basically, they don't make them anymore because in their eyes there's no demand. They will supply parts. In fact, they mailed me prints for the LKM 90 and LK 90, the two basic model numbers. I just scaled off those prints to get what I've got.

You made some improvements in the basic design?

I'm using a sealed roller bearing instead of a ball bearing on the connecting rod so there's better support and no maintenance. And I'm going to eliminate the clutch by using a DC electric motor with a foot pedal to control the speed. The direct drive makes it simpler and there are fewer parts to wear out, and less maintenance. I did buy the clutch castings from Jim, and Clay Cook can line them with a Kevlar material, instead of the old brake lining material or whatever they used originally. I think direct drive is the way to go.

How much do you have invested in the new hammer?

To date I've spent about $2000, and I will probably have $5000 or $6000 in it when I'm done. I did call in some favors from friends for the machining but otherwise I've done it all myself.

How did you make the arms, and what are they made from?

The arms are made from 3/8 inch thick, cold-rolled, picked and oiled,

Close up shows the connecting rod assembly from Jim Hervatin

How to Build a "Yoder"

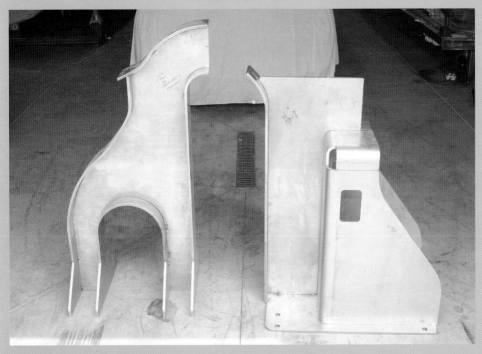

Neal's Yoder uses arms built from 3/8 inch steel plate, all laser cut and formed in a brake. The original Yoder drawings were used, and then extended six inches.

More of Neal's Yoder-in-the-making. Cast clutch, connecting rod, lower tool support and spring are from Jim Hervatin. Rough cut shrinking dies are an extra set that Neal purchased from another metal shaper. Neal had the guides fabricated and machined based on the Yoder drawings.

mild steel. I had all the parts laser cut. All the webbing parts are 3/8 too. Basically, the parts are an H-beam. I had to "bump brake" the steel that wraps the webbing, to get it to match the radius of the center web. Eventually all those seams will be fully welded. The center column will be 24 by 24 inches, and eight feet tall, made from the same 3/8 inch material. I'm going to use a five foot base on the bottom. This one will have a little more reach, six inches deeper than the original, just so you can get in there with bigger pieces.

So could anybody do this?

Anybody with the ability to do the machine work and welding. You need to be patient, you can't be in a hurry. What you're trying to duplicate is a big, heavy cast piece. It's big and clunky and heavy for a reason. If you can get parts flame cut or laser cut, that helps too. Part of this I figured out just by calling around. Scott Knight was very helpful, Fay Butler was nice, Jim answered questions and then let me drive down to see his hammer. It's a matter of finding the right people.

71

No, it's not a power hammer. Yet, most shapers agree that when it comes to buying power tools, a Pullmax is one of the best investments you can make.

shoes, or plow shares, or work a set of closed dies.

"When the country made the transition from carriages to autos, they discovered a need for a more durable body," explains Fay Butler. "Amesbury, Massachusetts was the Detroit of the carriage industry at that time. The Pettingell company was located there and supplied the carriage companies with wood-working equipment." As the industry made the transition from carriages to automobiles, and from wood to steel, it was only

Crank-operated hammers added speed to the process but the constant vibrations shortened the life of the mechanical linkage. Inventors began to experiment with springs as a means of isolating the ram from the rest of the machine, but it wasn't until Thomas Shaw tried using a semi-elliptical spring and leather strapping that the modern ram support mechanism was invented. Douglas Freund in his book, *Pounding Out The Profits*, gives Shaw credit for the first-such spring mechanism and dates the original patent to February 27, 1866.

Mr. Shaw's drive mechanism did more than isolate the linkage from the hammer. The elliptical spring and leather strapping allowed the head to drop free onto the anvil, producing a powerful "dead blow."

"MODERN" POWER HAMMERS

If you look at one of those early Shaw designs, what you see is a spring and strapping system nearly identical to that used by both Pettingell and Yoder. While the Yoder seems to be the better known hammer, it was Pettingell who first made a crank-operated power hammer designed to shape sheet metal rather than horse

Though the motor is mounted up above the machine and drive to the hammer is by belt, the Pettingell is functionally very similar to the Yoder. Available in a variety of sizes, this is one of the largest hammers that Pettingell sold.

natural that Pettingell would continue to supply the evolving industry with the tooling they needed for the new materials and manufacturing processes.

To quote Fay again, "The power hammer they developed evolved from the blacksmith hammer. Compared to a blacksmith hammer it had more throat and more speed. At one time they were a huge company, building power and hand rotary beading machines, and all kinds of equipment. The Yoder design evolved from the Pettingell design. Yoder was successful at getting a lot of government contracts. Almost all the Yoders you see now are military surplus, though some come from aircraft companies. Pettingell sold hammers primarily to automobile-related companies."

Current Power Hammer Options

Bill Hacker, long-time employee of Yoder, confirms what Fay has to say about the Yoder hammers. "We must have sold at least a two thousand Yoders during the Second World War. I remember we had them lined up in the main bay being assembled and there were always 25 or 30 there at any one time. But the sales tapered off in the later 1940s and early 1950s."

"The government bought a lot of those, the rest went to companies like Boeing and Douglas and all the rest. The last one we sold was about five or six years ago, it went to a Korean aircraft company and cost $50,000, plus extra for the dies."

Current options for shapers and fabricators looking for a power hammer include used Yoders, parts for which can still be obtained from Yoder or

from Jim Hervatin in Missouri. In fact, Jim will sell you many of the rough-castings you need for the mechanical end of a Yoder. Used Pettingells are also available though there doesn't seem to be an underground of enthusiasts producing replacement parts.

A complete power hammer kit is available from Cal Davis, classes are offered as well. Don't neglect to check out the tool offerings found on metalshapers.org

Whether you buy a real Yoder and do a lengthy restoration, or a new kit from Cal Davis, will depend on your budget for both time and money, and your mechanical aptitude. The important thing isn't which one you buy, but rather that you take the time to decide whether or not one of these labor savers is right for your shop. Called the "helper with no bad habits" a power hammer can shrink or stretch - and do it quicker than a dozen shapers working by hand.

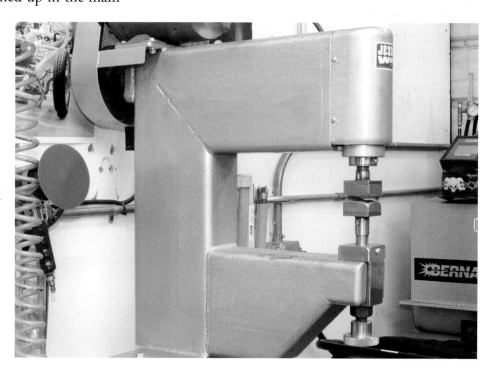

This small hammer is a one-off built by Loren Richards for Rob Roehl.

Art from Italy

Hand Built Panel for a Hand Built Car

Installing a patch panel in an old roadster might seem like the simplest of jobs. Unless the car in question is a rare 1948 AlfaRomeo with an aluminum body by Pininfarina, one of only two built and the only one surviving.

"Originally these cars were hammered out from sheet aluminum by hand," explains Mike Pavletic, "and planished to eliminate the rough surface. We're going to make the rear body panel out of 1100 aluminum. Essentially that is pure aluminum. The gauge of aluminum we're using is the same gauge as the rest of the body - .050

Once Mike stripped off all the old filler, he found an old poorly done repair made up of three separate pieces. Mike also had to cut out the support structure from inside the trunk so he cold fabricate, and finish, the new panel. Once the panel work is done he will fabricate a new support structure.

inch. That's what I'm using because that's probably what the car is made with; those panels are really soft. I don't use a buck for a project like this. If you have a piece to go by you don't need a buck. The existing piece becomes the buck. Sometimes you end up with more time and money in the buck than the part."

CUT THE SHEET

Mike starts by measuring the old piece and then figures out how to compensate for any shrinking that needs to be done. The lines he draws on the new piece show where the shrinking die will stop (at the first line) and where the area of maximum crown is (between the two lines). "You get an edge or shelf at the edge of the die," says Mike, "and that will be the area of maximum crown."

After two sessions of shrinking, with checking between, Mike declares it's time to do just one more bit of shrinking so the limit of the area affected by the die is right on the line closest to the edge. Then it's time to stretch the area where the panel starts to turn under to get it to roll a bit more.

After the shrinking and the first round of stretching, the piece is coming around. Mike pulls the edge up more, so it rolls more, and that flattens the new piece slightly. "This metal is still pretty soft, even after I've shaped it" explains Mike. "If I had done this on a little hand shrinker, cold-shrinking, the piece would end up a lot more brittle than when you use shrinking dies in a hammer."

Mike explains that sometimes you need to trust your eye. "The original panel is so rough that I'm going to 'follow my eye' more than the shape of the original piece." The first stretching dies that Mike uses are pretty sharp. After getting enough roll in the area of maximum radius, Mike changes to stretching dies for a low crown. With these dies Mike works the entire panel to put a soft crown in the whole thing.

Mike uses lots of test fits, (note the picture of the panel from the inside). At this point the

No paper pattern is used here, Mike simply measures and cuts the sheet of aluminum. He marks the edge of the area he will shrink on the new panel.

The aluminum for the patch is the same thickness as that on the car. Note the guide marks on the metal.

Mike encourages the metal to take on the proper shape with a little "armstrong" work.

This is what our piece looks like after two rounds of shrinking...

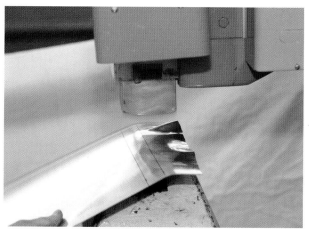

More shrinking is required, here you can see how the dies raise a "pucker" of metal...

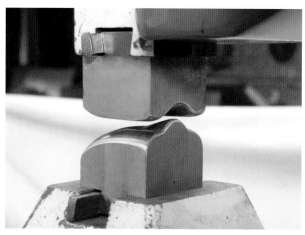

...in these familiar thumbnail dies. Before the test fit Mike will pass the panel through the dies one more time.

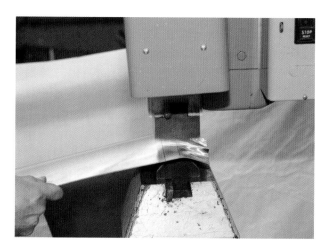

...and then knock it down as the sheet is withdrawn.

Here Mike lays the old lower-panels on top of the new panel to check the fit and the way the panel rolls at the edge.

Another look at the panel, note how the whole piece has picked up a crown.

panel needs a little more shrinking, so Mike changes dies again and takes the puckers out of the edge. Then he checks the fit again and trims off the excess. The piece is getting close but still needs to wrap a little tighter to the upper framework, "but that's just a matter of form, not shape," explains Mike.

FINISH IT ON THE PLANISHING HAMMER

"Now we can finish it off with the planishing hammer," says Mike. "With aluminum, you can do a lot of shaping with the planishing hammer because the metal is so soft. With the planishing hammer we're getting a little more crown across the panel, but mostly we're eliminating all the low spots that were left from the power hammer." With a sharper die in the planishing hammer, Mike finishes the crowned area or cor-

The first test fit simply confirms that Mike has the panel moving in the right direction.

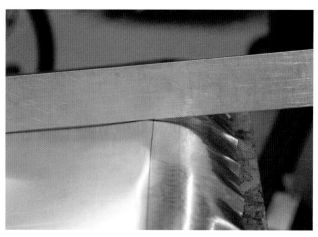

This is a look at the bottom edge after the sharper stretching dies were used to help establish the roll where the panel turns under.

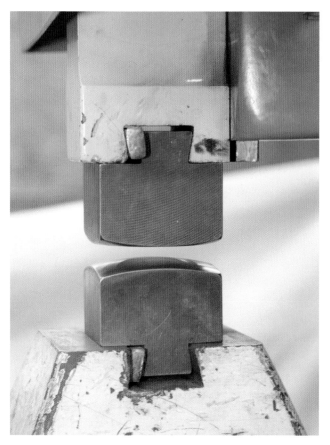

This is the second set of stretching dies used early in the project, the "low-crown dies" used to begin putting a crown in the entire piece."

The second set of stretching dies (shown at left) are used here to begin creating crown across the entire piece.

Note the amount of crown in the panel, created in just a few minutes.

...in order to create more top-to-bottom crown.

Most of the crown is side to side. Though hard to see, there is some crown top-to-bottom.

Next comes a test fit.

Mike does more work with the same dies...

Note how close the piece is fitting the back of the car when viewed from the inside.

ner at the bottom of the panel. These dies match the inside radius at that part of the panel.

Numerous test fits follow, then a change to flatter dies, now he works to finish the upper edge. The finished panel has a little more crown than the original, (when viewed the short way). But, as Mike notes, "it's hard to know how accurate the original panel was."

FOLD THE EDGE

Now the top of the old panel is clamped in place and used to draw the fold line on the new panel. "Then I add close to 1/2 inch for the folded metal even though it measures 3/8 inch," says Mike. Then he marks a series of dashes, rolls the tape out to make a nice curved line, and cuts it with a snips.

After the piece is trimmed to fit, Mike checks the position of the fold line, then starts the folding with a pliers. "With steel I use a die on the Pullmax to score the metal, but the aluminum is so soft it's easy to over-score the metal. It's safer to just do it by hand."

Of course the lip that Mike bends into the panel tends to straighten it out, which means he needs to shrink it more. Once the crown is re-established he checks the fit again, and then bends the flange over a stake. After another test fit Mike tightens up the fold, "As you hammer the fold flat on the car, it affects the fit between the trunk lid and this panel. So it's best to get it as tight as you can before you start welding the panel in place."

The nearly finished panel is a little asymmetrical. But this is, after all, a hand built car. After comparing the new panel to the old, Mike decides that the shape is true to the original so if the shape is a little unusual that's OK.

To double check the fit of the panel before the welding begins, Mike and his son Ryan set the trunk lid in place. Once it's determined that the fit of the trunk lid to the panel is good, then the trunk lid is lifted off and Mike does some minor trimming necessary to make the new panel fit.

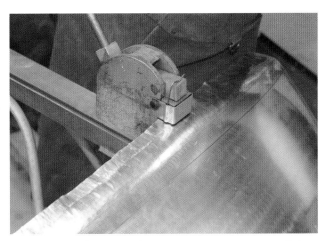

After using the power hammer to remove most of the distortion left from the thumbnail dies, Mike uses the small shrinker to tighten up the roll...

...so it better matches the existing body panels.

Now Mike can mark the panel prior to trimming and folding.

Trimming is done in various steps, followed by...

...another test fit...

...followed by finish work on the planishing hammer. This will add slightly to the panel's crown.

Before welding Mike de-burrs the edges and cleans them with Acetone on a rag. The panel is welded in place with the TIG welder using a 1/16th inch pure tungsten. Mike uses a TIG welder with the amperage control on the handle, not on the pedal, set at 75 amps.

Welding this piece of aluminum in place is a little difficult, partly because the original body panels are thin and partly because there is corrosion on the original panels that makes it hard to weld. During the welding, Mike notes that, "They no longer recommend forming a "ball" on the end of the tungsten when you're welding aluminum. The standards have changed."

THE FINISH WORK

When it comes to finishing the metal, Mike avoids what is commonly called metal finishing, because, "it ruins the integrity of the metal. I tend to work the metal as much as I can without doing a lot of filing. I try to leave the metal as thick as possible." He also notes that, "No matter what level you take the piece to, you're going to have to finish it more after it's in place, just because of the distortion from welding."

At this point the panel is in place, with only the finish work to do. For finishing, Mike puts crown back in with the Chicago Pneumatic air-planishing hammer. This planishing, or finishing, is done in two sessions, one with flat dies, the last with slightly more crowned dies.

INTERVIEW WITH MIKE PAVLETIC

Mike, can we start with some background on you and how you became a metal fabricator?

I was hired to work in my cousin's body shop in high school, prepping and painting cars. From there I did the route of regular body shops for five or six years, before getting into high end stuff, the high dollar European cars, the money cars. I did that for ten years. When I was working in somebody else's shop I was mostly painting. I moved home to my own shop 15 years ago. It was street rod work, I did the paint and the whole car. Then a couple of years ago I built this building and now metal work is pretty much all that I do.

The work of the planishing hammer leaves Mike with a panel that is nearly perfect and correctly crowned just enough in both directions.

A test fit shows the new panel to be a very good match with the other existing panels.

Mike finished the area of maximum radius with the planishing hammer and a sharper die than what was used earlier.

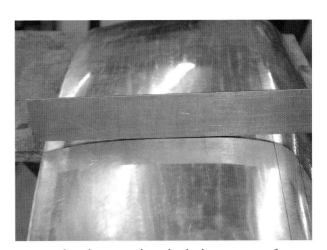

A straight edge is used to check the amount of crown from top to bottom.

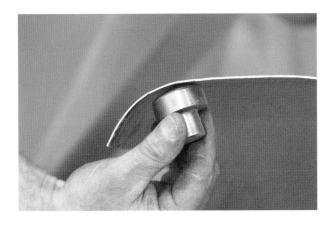

Here you can see the lower die used to finish the area seen above.

The small hand-shrinker is used to tighten up the roll slightly on the bottom of the panel.

At this point Mike checks the fit and the amount of crown against the original inner structure.

Now the piece is clamped in place so Mike can mark the fold line.

The position of the fold line, and the amount of metal to leave for the fold itself, are checked against the upper part of the "original" panel.

I could metal-finish the cars clear back when I was painting. But I wasn't hired to do metal work. I'm lucky, if I see somebody do something I can usually pick it up and that's how I learned a lot of this.

At some point you took a class from Fay Butler?

Yes, because otherwise you read magazines and books, and you buy tools. Then you get an English wheel and you aren't sure how to use it. Fay can impart knowledge that you can't acquire any place else, at least at that time you couldn't. I started to understand things like 'working past the metal's elastic limit.' Once you learn all the terms and metallurgy you know what's happening at the atomic level of the steel. Fay's a good teacher.

You said you started with a wheel and now you have a power hammer. Can you explain the advantages of each and why you bought the tools you did?

I built a wheel and learned how to use it, I didn't think it was that difficult to use. Then I went to Fay's and used his power hammers and saw that they were more efficient. So then I sold the English wheel and bought a power hammer. I tell a lot of guys to buy a wheel. It's affordable, you can wheel out a panel and have it nice and not need any filler. Some of the schools are starting to cover the use of a wheel. You supply all the power to the wheel though, with a power hammer you use the motor to supply the force.

Now you do most of your work on a power hammer?

Yes, it's a tremendous tool. Part of it is learning the use of the hammer. Instead of hammering a fender over a sand bag and then smoothing it out with a wheel, you can shape it nice and easy with the hammer. Most of the pieces I make don't even need to be planished.

What's the minimum tooling a person needs to do advanced-level shaping?

An English wheel and a Pullmax would be a good start. And some kind of welder.

Here you can see both the fold line and the trim line.

...before finishing up the fold with a hammer working over a stake.

Mike's son Chase steadies the panel as the beginning of the fold is formed by hand.

The panel can now be slid down into place...

To re-create some of the crown, Mike runs the folded area through the hand shrinker...

...before being welded to the other panels with the TIG welder.

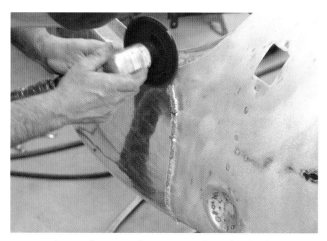

A grinder and coarse disc are used to do the first step in finishing the welded seam...

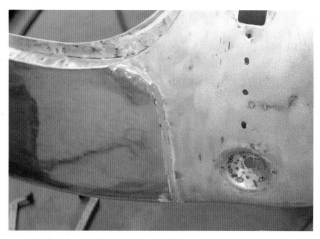

...which leaves the seam in the condition seen here. The other effect of the welding is to eliminate some of the top-to-bottom crown.

To finish the seam and re-crown the panel Mike uses an air planishing hammer, equipped initially with fairly flat dies (shown), then with more crowned dies.

Bigger pieces mean more seams, is a TIG welder essential?

You don't have to have a TIG welder. Lots of guys only have gas welders and they do fine. The TIG makes things easier. It's a matter of what you've learned and what you can afford. The gas weld is annealed so it's soft and you can hammer-weld it and end up with a nice seam. I started with a Dillon gas-welding outfit. It only uses 4-5 pounds of pressure for both gasses so you're less likely to blow through when you're welding aluminum.

What about bucks, how often do you use one?

I personally don't get the type of jobs that need a buck. I don't use them very often. Part of it depends on the work that comes through your door. They have a place, but they're not always a necessity.

Advanced Sheet metal means bigger, more complex shapes. Can you talk about the seams. How does a person decide where to put the seams and how does he or she decide how many pieces to make an individual part out of?

That should probably be determined by the size of the panel and the access you have to the area where you want to put the seam. I'm inclined to put them in a crowned area rather than a flat area. The crowned area has more strength, it won't warp as much and you can run the planishing hammer over it when you're done. Basically, it comes down to your skill level.

Aluminum versus steel, do you prefer one over the other?

Depends on what the project is. Whatever work I get, that's what I do. The Alfa is made from aluminum, I don't have a problem with either metal.

Is there one skill that's more important than the others?

You need a whole combination of skills. On a personal level, you need the drive to do it. You work by yourself so you have to be a good problem solver.

Is a good eye essential to metal shaping?

Yes, definitely. If you look at something and it doesn't look right it probably isn't. You need to make a correction. I tell my sons, "if it looks right it is right."

Are there abilities that people need, that if they don't have them, will hold them back from bigger projects. Where do people fall down in terms of skills or abilities?

There are really only two things they need, the experience of doing it and the knowledge. It helps to get the knowledge at a seminar or from a book. Then you have to apply it. If a person is trying to learn it too quickly, or if they read all these books and then just want to run out and start making panels then they can get in over their head. The more knowledge you can acquire, the less steep the learning curve will be.

Don't expect to start out and right away be able to do it as well as someone who's done it for 20 years. Set your goals high, but not so high that you fail. Give yourself time to learn. Be patient, it doesn't happen overnight.

The small air planishing hammer is designed to he hand-held so panels can be finished on the car.

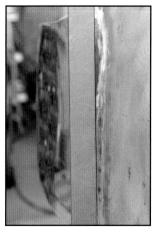

Before and after shots use a ruler to show how much crown the panel picked up as a result of Mike's work with the hand-held planishing hammer.

Here's the old Alfa with the "patch panel" installed. Although the gauge and alloy used in the new panel are very close to the old panels, it was still hard to weld due to inevitable corrosion and inconsistencies in the thickness of the original metal.

Chapter Seven

Henry J

The Saga Continues

The saga of building my Henry J has gone on so long I could use the experience to write a tome the size of *Moby Dick*. For now though let's just take a look at how a non-professional sheet metal worker partnered up with a professional so that they could make a tunnel and a bell housing cover.

To back up a bit, an earlier sheet metal guy installed a new floor and firewall a few years back, but didn't finish the floor. Thus I was left with two options, either take the car to a different fabricator, or try to somehow do at least part of it myself.

I opted for door number two, partly just to

Perhaps not a thing of beauty, but the floor is covered. By making the bucks in my small garage and taking those to the shop of a professional sheet metal fabricator, I was able to keep the car at home and do some of the work myself, but it took longer than it would have to just haul the car to a shop and say, "do it."

keep control of the project, partly to save funds, and partly just for the pleasure of doing it myself.

The professional sheet metal craftsman I chose to work with on this second occasion is Rob Roehl, long-time fab guy at Donnie Smith Custom Cycles. Though Rob and I both live in the Minneapolis/St. Paul metro area, that doesn't mean we are close neighbors. Rather than bring the car to Rob, or bring Rob to the car, I decided to make a buck so Rob could form the tunnel and then return it to me for final trimming and fitment in the car.

The plan worked reasonably well and might work in other situations where you don't want to trailer the car to a shop and leave it, even for a few days. And, as I said, it certainly does involve the owner in the project.

This is really just an elaboration on the methods Steve Davis used in the short how to sequence seen at the front of the book. As always, the key is patience. Mostly patience in making a good buck, because that will determine the accuracy of your sheet metal. Any time and effort spend on the front end making sure the buck is accurate, will help ensure that the actual sheet metal piece fits correctly. And though it sounds too obvious to say, fitment is the whole key here. Otherwise you are left "adjusting" the sheet metal once you get it back to your own shop. An accurate fit of the new piece(s) will also make the welding about ten times easier. Time spent making a good buck, and making sure the sheet metal fits before starting any welding, will pay big dividends later.

In my case, I started with "muffler strap" to make crude hoops that arched up from one side of the floor to the other - you have to start someplace. Then, when those hoops looked workable, I bought some heavier strap at the hardware store and bent it to match the muffler strap. During the process I often used a long level as a straight edge to make sure the tops of the three hoops were level and would define a line that ran downhill toward the rearend. For some of this I used light board purchased at the drug store, and later I used "butcher paper" from (yes) the butcher shop. In hindsight I liked the butcher paper better.

continued, page 90

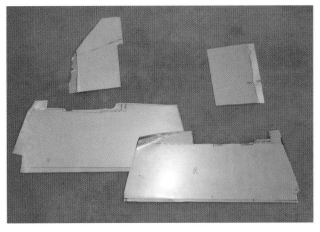

Making what I call the toe boards, shown here, was easy as they have no real shape. I made cardboard templates, and used them to cut out the steel as shown...

...then weld them in place on the left and right hand side of the floor.

For the tunnel I started by making loops out of very light material...

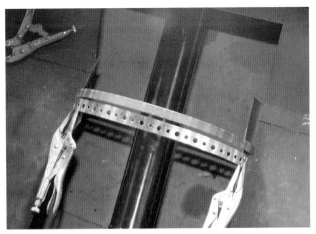

...then when the loops seemed to have the right shape I made a heavier loop from 1/8 inch thick material from the hardware store.

Here's the finished buck, all the loops tied together with a straight backbone. Note the kink in the floor between the second and third loop.

I checked the "run" of the loops often with this straight edge. In hindsight more loops might have been a good idea.

Time now to cover the loops with paper, cutting and slitting where necessary to make the paper fit the buck.

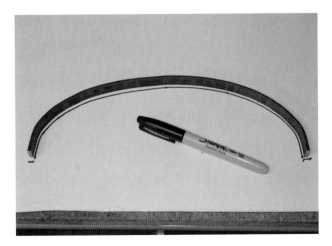

One of the tricks I've learned - put the loop on paper, outline it with a marker, then flip it end to end. Does it still match the outline drawn on the paper?

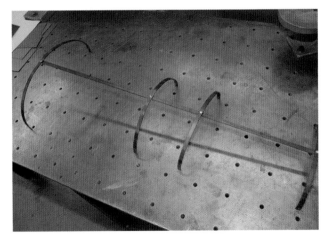

Once the paper template was complete I could bring both the buck and the template to the fab shop.

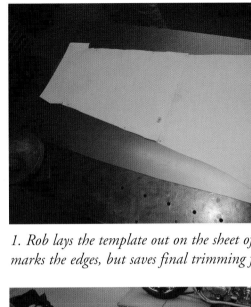

1. Rob lays the template out on the sheet of steel, and marks the edges, but saves final trimming for later.

3. Without access to a fancy rolling machine, Rob decides to create the tunnel with a bit of old skool ingenuity - basically he moves the sheet relative to the pipe each time he does a bend.

2. The key is this surface table, a big piece of pipe and a couple of clamps.

4. Close up shows the stepped clamp and how it's mounted to one of the threaded holes in the surface table.

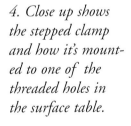

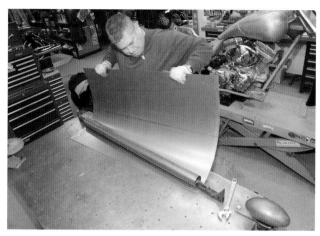

1. Rob cut out the 16 gauge steel a little too big, then locked it in place on the surface table as shown. Note that the centerline is marked out.

2. Forming the tunnel required...

3. ...a pair of strong arms and...

4. ...repositioning of the sheet metal numerous times.

As Steve Davis says (Chapter Two), "the paper predicts the shape." I tried to make sure the paper did in fact represent the shape I wanted and that it was trimmed pretty accurately. The buck served as both a way to create a template for shaping the steel, and later as a checking device so Rob could tell if he was creating too little or too much radius.

Forming a tunnel looks pretty simple, and for the most part it is. The decreasing radius from one end to the other does present a challenge however. There are sheet metal rolling machines that can be used to create a piece like this, with a radius that decreases from one end to the other. Of course Rod didn't have one of those. Actually, I think Rob kind of enjoyed the idea of creating most of the basic shape with nothing fancier that a surface table, a long pipe, a couple of clamps, and plenty of good old elbow grease.

Rob did use an English wheel, as shown, to smooth out wrinkles in the metal, and to raise the metal just a bit more in some areas. And the slap hammer and dolly came in handy to help smooth

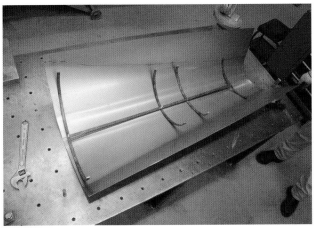

At this point the buck becomes a checking device, we need more radius.

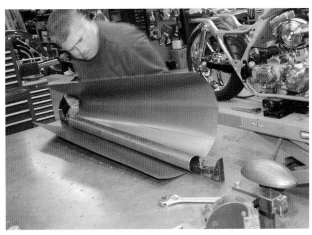

A larger diameter tube would have been nice, as there would have been fewer kinks in the steel.

Created as shown - with the armstrong method.

Rob checks the progress, we are getting pretty close now.

Repositioning the sheet metal meant releasing the two clamps, sliding the steel under the pipe, and then pinching it in place again.

Which means he can trim off the excess, though he still leaves a little extra metal for me to trim later.

Though not essential, the English wheel is useful...

And if the wheel won't eliminate the kind, there's always the old fashioned hammer and dolly method.

...both to help raise the metal slightly and to eliminate the kinks in the tunnel where it was forced up against the tube.

For the latest part of the wheel work Rob uses a very flat lower wheel as shown...

Here you can see the sharp bends which are most obvious at the tunnel's edge.

...and runs the tunnel the long way through the wheel.

the edge of the metal at the big end.

FINAL ADJUSTMENTS

The hardest part was doing the final adjusting of the new tunnel once I got it back to my garage, so it would match the opening in the floor. You see, the edges on either side of the drive shaft, aren't strictly straight, which forced me to slit the sides of the tunnel as I tried to make it fit. Also, the tail end, where the tunnel meets the floor, was a little tough as the radius flares out and becomes almost flat where it meets the old floor.

At this point the tunnel is deemed finished, or as finished as it can be without having the car nearby for a check of the fitment.

Forcing the lower edge of the tunnel up against the flange in the floor so we could weld it in place was tough as well. With help from a couple of other friends, however, we did force the tunnel up against the lip in the floor. If I did this again I might try to design the tunnel so it slipped inside the flange at the edge of the floor instead of outside. We had trouble welding the tunnel in place simply because the fit wasn't always perfect. In some spots we had to go back and grind out the welds, improve the fit, and then weld that area again.

Poor fitment might be the bad news, but the good news is the fact that the tunnel is in. Not to use this as an excuse, but in truth, once the seam is sealed and the carpet goes in, no one will ever see the tunnel again. So if you want to do part of the sheet metal fabrication yourself, but don't think you have the skills to actually make the piece from scratch, consider this hybrid option, which utilizes the energy of two individuals instead of one.

Here's the first test fit, and it's pretty close. I did some slitting at the back and along the side where there's a little kink in the opening. It might have been easier to do this as 2 pieces.

Here's the buck, a little light, but adequate to the job. Wires are tack welded together, washers and pins provide a means of locating the paper template.

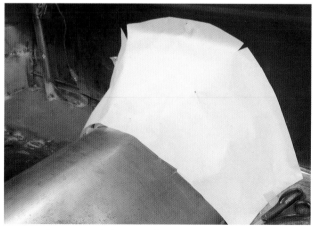

Here's the paper template trimmed and mounted on the buck.

A test fit to see if the template actually fits the hole.

Forming the buck for the bell housing cover proved a bit more challenging than the one I crafted for the tunnel. Because whereas the tunnel doesn't have much real shape, the bell housing cover would have a definite crown.

The trip took me to the proverbial hardware store where I bought some light round stock, about 3/32 inches in diameter. Welding rod likely would have worked just as well. My buck ended up being a little fragile, but on the other hand the light material was pretty easy to bend.

As you can see I did form a crown by forming an arch in both the wires that go side to side, and those that run the length of the car. After tack welding them together I welded small washers in place so I could punch holes in the template and use pins to register the template on the buck. Next came the butcher paper, mentioned earlier, cut and slit until it fit really nice on the buck.

Once at the sheet metal shop, Rob used my template to cut out the shape from a piece of 18 gauge mild steel. Cutting is done on the band saw, though nearly any decent means of cutting could be used. As always, Rob cuts the piece bigger than it really needs to be.

The shaping starts with the armstrong method followed by a quick check against the buck. As stated earlier, this piece has some definite shape, which did require some stretching and shrinking as well.

The stretching is done with the English wheel. First Rob runs the piece through the long way, then checks it, runs it through again and begins to work on the crown in the center more by running the center part of the bell housing cover through at a 45 degree angle, then turning the piece 90 degrees before running it through again. By going back and forth like this Rob creates a nice symmetrical crown and minimizes any track marks that might be left on the metal by the wheel.

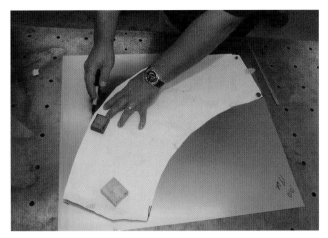

The template is used to mark out the steel.

More armstrong work...

Rob cuts the sheet metal just a little too big...

...followed by a check against the buck...

...and starts the bending on the edge of the bench.

...and some work on the wheel to begin raising the center of the bell housing cover.

Progress so far...

Now Rob works more in the center of the cover, running the metal through at a 45 degree angle, then turning it 90 degrees and running it through again.

...and another check against the buck.

Followed by more work done working the long way.

The ruler or straightedge is a good way to check the amount of crown that's been created by the stretching in the English wheel.

Though it's subtle, there is definitely some crown being formed here.

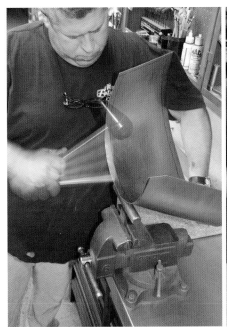  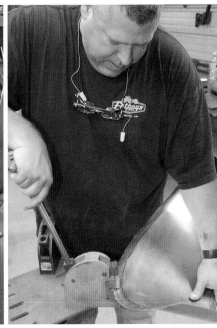

The beginnings of the flange on either side of the cover...

...is created by working the edge over a dolly with a plastic hammer.

Rob uses the small stretcher to flare out the flange without splitting the sheet metal.

You don't want to go too far, and at this point Rob checks the cover against the buck pretty often.

By using the buck on the outside, it's easy to check the location of the flanges.

1. Sheet metal doesn't like to move too fast, here Rob is massaging it a bit more with the plastic hammer...

2. ...followed by more time in the jaws of the stretcher.

3. This special roller for the English wheel comes in very handy to finish the flange at the back of the cover.

4. Another check shows the bell housing cover to be almost finished.

3. To add more crown through the center Rob puts the nearly finished piece back in the wheel.

The flange at the front and back of the housing cover is created mostly with a soft-faced plastic hammer working the metal over a home-made T-dolly.

As the pictures show, finishing the cover is a matter of carefully stretching and shrinking the metal, with plenty of checks against the buck, for good measure. The flanges at the side are the easiest part, formed with a hammer working over another dolly mounted in the vise.

Back at my elaborate home shop, the initial check showed a cover that fit pretty darned good, even if it did sit up a little too far. That part was easily remedied, I just trimmed the flanges at the sides off and formed new ones, which essentially lowered the whole thing by about a half or three-quarter inch. Once I had it low enough, I used a couple of sheet metal screws on either side to

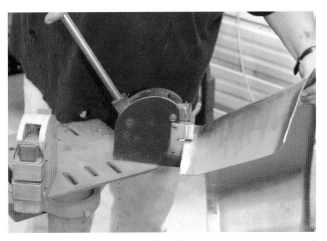

1. After running the smaller flange through the wheel Rob needs to shrink it back down a bit.

2. The big flange requires the opposite treatment.

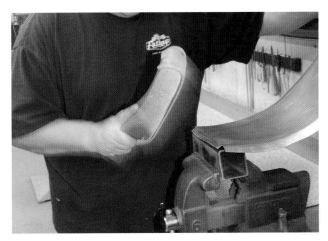

4. The flanges that meet the floor on either side of the cover are formed with a slap hammer and a very simple dolly.

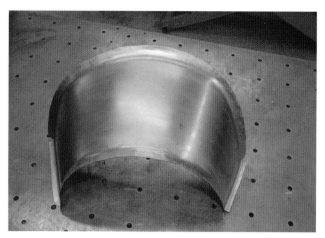

2. The finished cover, with an almost polished finished created by the English wheel.

1. Here you can see how the metal is folded over the edge of the dolly, and how the metal was cut out at the corner where the two flanges meet.

3. The first test fit of the cover in the car. Note the back flange it a bit high off the tunnel.

Finally, the welding begins. Note the small slits at the edge of the back flange - kind of a poor man's means of shrinking.

mount it solidly to the toe plates. Then I marked the outside of the big front flange where it overlapped the firewall, and the back of the smaller rear flange, where it overlapped the tunnel.

After pulling off the bell housing cover I trimmed both the firewall and the end of the tunnel to allow for about a quarter inch of overlap between the two surfaces. The front flange matched up to the surface of the firewall almost perfectly with no gaps. The smaller flange was another story however and was simply too big. Without a shrinker I simply slit the flange again and again and gently tapped the flange until the tunnel's flange fit snug up against edge of the tunnel.

Now I set the cover in place for the last time, put the sheet metal screws in place to pull it down nice and tight, and commenced to carefully weld all the seams.

And though the bell housing cover is the more complex piece to create, it turned out better than the tunnel. Maybe this is because it's a bit smaller, or because it butts up against pretty regular surfaces so there was less "adjusting" needed to make it fit perfectly.

At any rate, the two projects did turn out pretty well, and the car never left my shop.

Here's Bob at work welding the bell housing cover in place. Note the evenly spaced small welds.

Tack welds around the perimeter of the bell housing cover have all been filled in and merge to one seam.

As the story says, fitment is critical. Always take the time to make sure the two parts fit together with as much precision as possible. Don't just start welding in haste with the idea you will get it done faster that way.

101

Fender Fabrication

First You Have to Make the Buck

When Bruce Terry agreed to make a demonstration fender for the book, he decided to go all the way. The fender isn't a little shorty bobber fender, but rather a full fender formed with the help of a buck.

Bruce starts this project by measuring the radius of a nearby motorcycle wheel, and comes up with a 12 inch measurement.

A piece of wire is shaped and used as a profile or guide, Bruce explains as he does, "you can

Perhaps a bit over the top for a basic fabrication book, the shaping of this fender includes the construction and use of a buck, a useful lesson for anyone contemplating more elaborate shaping projects.

draw a line with the guide and then flip the guide over and see if it's symmetrical. I decide the depth of the fender is 3-1/2 inches, so then we can draw in the bottom of the fender, the lip."

DRAW IT ON PAPER

Working from these known dimensions Bruce draws out a full size fender, and from that starts the construction of the buck. The side rails, made from 1-1/8 inch steel straps, are the first parts to be formed. Making the buck turns into a fabrication lesson all its own, complete with a shrinking lesson for the side rails and the creation of a bending jig that makes it relatively easy to shape a series of identical curved ribs.

Building the buck is made easier by the full size drawing. During the construction Bruce works hard to ensure that the cross braces and the ribs are identical in dimension and shape. Much of the steel used for the buck is hot-rolled, which means the slag must be ground off the outside. "The slag is super hard carbon," explains Bruce. "It will contaminate the welds and it also gums up the jaws of the shrinker, which is why some guys buy nothing but cold-rolled steel."

"A lot of guys over-weld everything," says Bruce. "But all that welding causes too much warpage, so I try to go with lighter welds as I weld in the cross braces and the ribs." One of the last parts of the puzzle to figure out is the tail of the fender. Once Bruce decides on a shape he comes up with a way to incorporate that shape into the buck. "I think the way I'm going to approach this is to form the center part of the fender first, then the two sides, so it will be made from a total of three pieces."

THE PAPER TEMPLATE

"Its amazing how much shape there is in this fender," explains Bruce. "Anything that has an arch to it and is a compound curve has a lot of shape. The paper template shows you how much shape the piece has, and can be used as a pattern when you cut the metal. The degree of overlap where I do the slits shows how much shrinking you will have to do. If there were areas where you had to cut slots and the slots in the template end

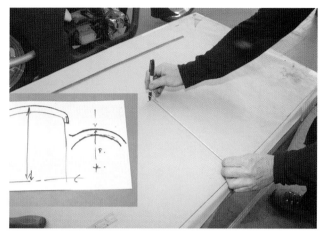

Now I'm ready to draw the layout full size with accurate radius and dimensions.

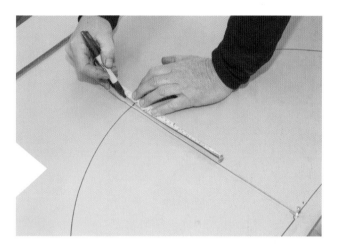

The radius of the fender is important so allow for enough clearance between the fender and the tire.

Here the exterior radius (O. D.) is drawn to illustrate the tire size.

103

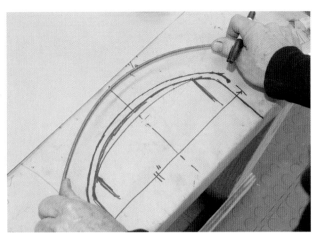

Using a steel rod, a smooth natural shape is created to establish the top radius of the fender.

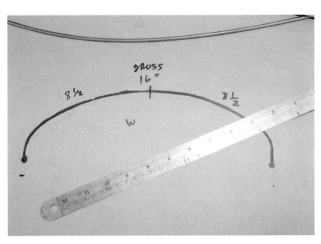

Then I measure out the full sized, cross section drawing in order to determine the materials needed.

Then we look at a cross section and note clearance on the top and sides of the tire.

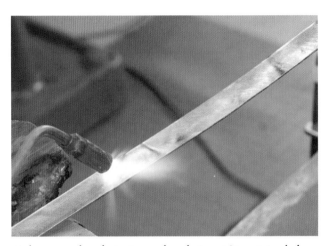

A large pushrod tip is used to bring 1/8 x 1 inch bar to red hot.

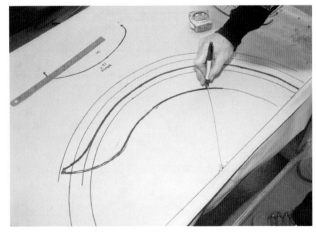

Now a cross section is drawn showing the stylish tail design.

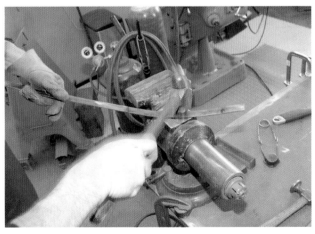

Here I am planishing/hammering the "cold" side of the bar to stretch the bar into the desired shape.

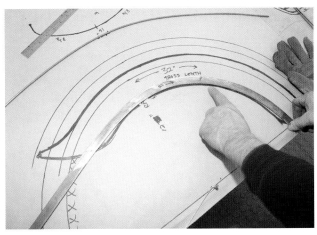

This bar is formed to fit the cross section drawing and will be used as one side of the station buck to be made.

Then the fabricated framework is checked against the cross section drawing.

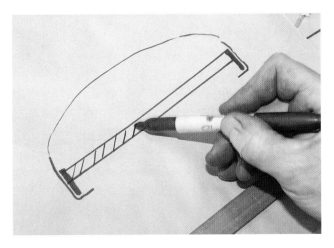

Now focusing on the buck design, a cross section drawing is being conceptualized.

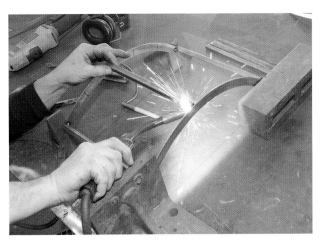

After cutting the square tubes I start to tack weld them in place.

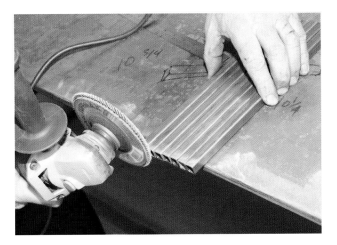

Here I am making sure the cross braces are all the same exact dimension.

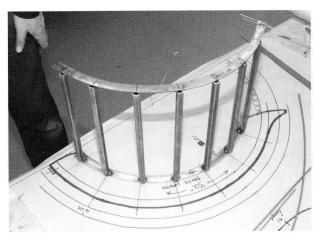

Now I check it all against the full-size drawing.

I modified the bending jig (seen on page 98) which is used as an aid in forming the many curved cross section pieces or ribs.

After bending I check the ribs against a line drawing made on the fabrication table.

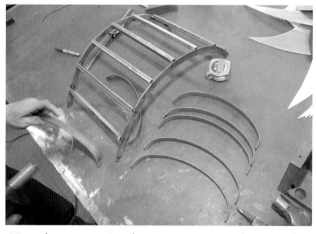

Now the corss section braces are coming along nicely.

up spread out, that would show the areas that need to be stretched."

The material is 3003 aluminum and Bruce anneals the aluminum in order to make it easier and faster to shape this fender. "You should almost be able to see through the layer of soot," says Bruce, "and then heat the metal enough that you burn off that soot. The soot is just a temperature indicator. The process will take the metal back to a dead-soft condition."

HAMMER ON

Though he starts the actual shaping with a plastic mallet, stretching the metal through the center, Bruce realizes right away that the creation of this fender will require a lot of shrinking as well. "Those little hand shrinkers are almost essential, they're really handy. You could make the piece with mostly stretching, but it's really a lot of hammering, a lot more work that way."

To eliminate most of the lumps left from the plastic mallet, Bruce uses a slap hammer and a post dolly and then moves to the English wheel.

"With the wheel, you have to understand the tracking, note the pattern. As I work the panel I never stop in the same place twice and then after running it through the wheel I turn the metal 90 degrees and go through the same process.

Time for a test fit, "at this point I have pretty good contact on center part of the ribs but not at the outer edges."

SHRINKING AND WHEELING

The next step is back to the shrinker, "what really accelerates the speed of the overall shaping is the shrinking," explains Bruce. "The wheel is nice because it makes the aluminum shiny so you can see what you're doing.

At this point we have good shape at the front and less shape farther back on the panel. Along the way Bruce does frequent test fits. At this point the center part of the fender is fitting better, though the tail needs to be stretched because it flares out,

As is common with most of these fabrication projects, the shape evolves slowly. To ensure he

continued, page 110

Now the backside of the ribs are welded from behind for strength and to be out of the way of the outer surface.

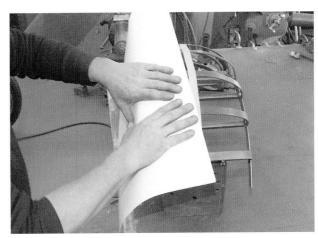

I'm using a flat piece of art paper which I tape to the buck...

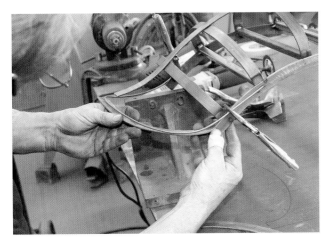

Now I shape the trail area using round rod to assist in achieving a smooth shape.

Next I pie-cut the paper...

Here the tail section of the buck is formed and welded in place with a short shape-support indicator.

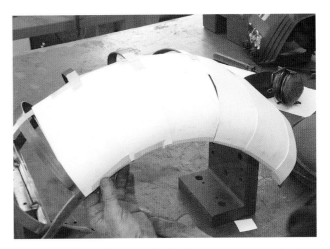

...so it will conform to the buck. Once removed, the template will help us determine the size of the aluminum sheet needed.

It is always best to go a little large when you cut out the actual raw panel.

Well, I need to hammer this H14 with a Teflon hammer in order to start the stretching process.

Time to anneal the sheet aluminum. I am using a dusting of acetylene smoke as a guide to the proper annealing temperature.

Focusing on the crown of the fender, I continue to hammer – thus stretching the annealed material.

Darn. That doesn't fit very well.

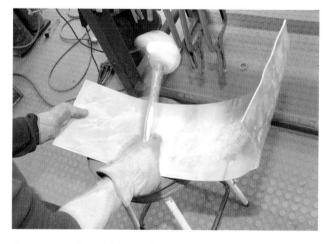

It is scary, but I know the stretching is happening.

Holding the panel flat you can see how much stretching has been achieved so far.

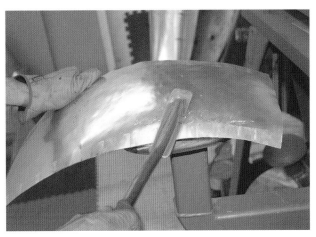

Next I smooth some of the bumps out with a lightweight slapping hammer I purchase from Ron Covell.

Let's keep going on the ends.

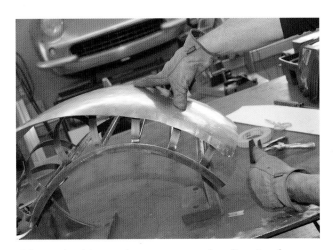

I keep checking to be sure we are heading in the right direction with our shape.

One way to speed up the process is to shrink down the edges with this economic and common shrinker tool.

A little wheel work will smooth out the lumps and add to the stretching.

The wheel smoothes things out nicely.

Now that I have the general shape I'm going to run this panel through the English wheel. The lines indicate a typical wheeling pattern.

Let's see if we can get it even smoother.

puts the fender on the buck in the same position each time, Bruce drills a hole and inserts a spring loaded Cleco.

With a combination of the English wheel and the small shrinker, Bruce creates more crown in the back of the fender, in the center. " I've marked the area with a marker. I'm' going to put it back on the wheel."

One of the hardest areas to shape is the tail, as Bruce explains, "this area is tough because it's an inverse compound curve." And for a really hard area like this Bruce brings out one of the oldest metal shaping tools around, the hollowed-out tree

I can also use this wheel to apply pressure, thus raising or stretching the panel into shape.

Look at all the shape we have established.

And then back to the shrinker.

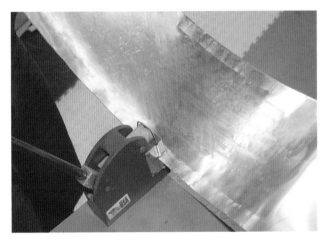

A little more shrinking along the edges will bring our panel into shape.

This tail section is a reverse compound shape. I need to stretch the bottom edge.

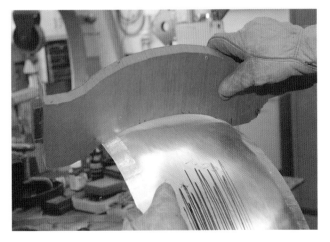

Let's check our shape with one of these cool shape transfer tools. The fender has a ways to go.

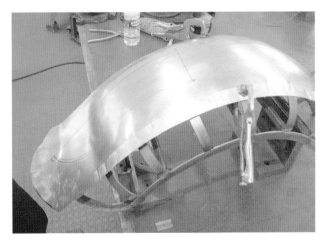

Looking good clamped in place.

Here I am using the wheel to help flip the tail section.

Here I'm still focusing on the tail section.

Yet, some more shrinking.

Using these cool post dollies from Canada I continue to shape the tail.

A short study to understand the movement of this complex shape change.

The inverse compound shape is the toughest of all. Time to go to the Ol' tree stump.

Looks like we have a long way to go.

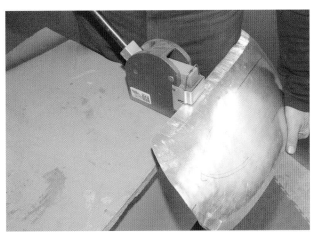

Pulling the radius around again with the shrinking tool.

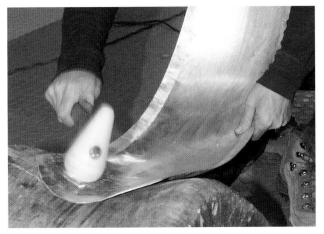

25 years ago I took a chainsaw to a stump to form this inverse curve.

This is feeling good now. The aluminum is getting smooth and shiny.

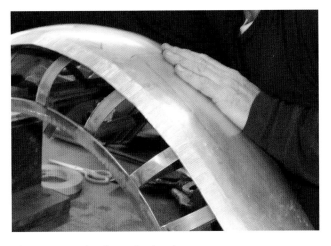

Once again back to the buck.

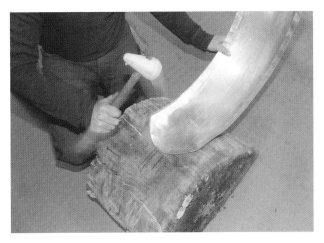

Thank goodness for the Ol' inverse curve stump tool.

Looking under the buck I can see I have a long way to go.

A few more stretching blows with a broader Teflon hammer.

Here I'm using the wheel to stretch and raise the panel.

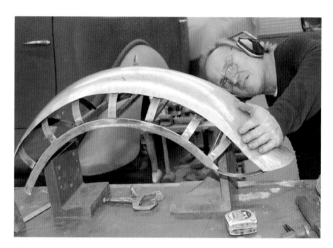

I can see now what I need to do. I need to raise the part under my hand and flip the tail farther.

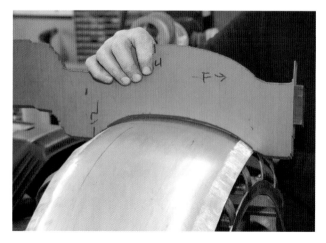

Let's check the cross section again with our handy curve gauge.

And back to the post dolly for more refinements.

114

Yet more slapping with the "Covell Slapper".

...a bit more slapping to flair the tail edge.

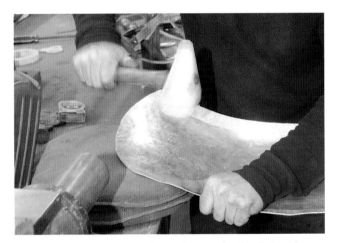

I'm moving the tail outbound over the lead shot bag.

The tail really flairs out at the bottom.

Now, about that tail area.......

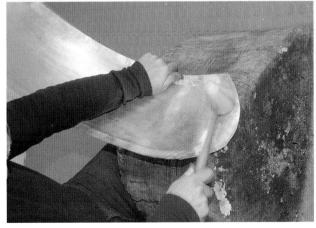

A bit more shaping on the stump.

Our fender top section is really coming into shape.

Just a bit more slapping on the post dolly.

Clamped into place and looking good. The panel fits on the buck nicely.

stump, explaining, "that stump has exactly the shape I want."

Hammering the fender over the stump is interspersed with more shrinker work and more time spent working the fender on the post dolly with a slapper.

Now it's time for more shrinker work and another test fit. "When I use the shrinker I always take a full depth shrink and then go back and take a half depth shrink." About this time Bruce decides that what he needs is "more flip at the end. Like I said, that tail is a very hard shape to create."

"Once you have a little experience you can gauge the progress by carefully looking over the piece, and checking it with your hand. The contour gauge (seen on page 104) is another good way to check the progress of the shape against the buck."

"You can move metal faster with a hammer than the wheel," explains Bruce, "so I'm going to raise metal at the transition area and then smooth it out with the post dolly, and then do another test fit."

This is the part of the project where it's a great deal of making small changes, checking, and then making additional small changes. The changes are often so subtle that they are hard to discern especially for the camera.

Bruce anneals the end of the fender again, (not shown) "otherwise the metal will work harden and then it will split." After annealing it's back to the post dolly. The slap hammer is a great tool. You can actually move the metal in a certain direction with the direction of your blows.

On page 115 you can see the "finished fender" and though there's still work to do our deadline requires this stopping point. Despite the fact that the fender isn't quite done, we have shown a variety of shaping methods, as well as the creation and use of a buck as a fabricating aid.

PART TWO:

INSTALLATION OF THE FENDER SIDES, AND INITIAL METAL FINISHING.

Finishing this fender meant adding the sides. Different fabricators might have slightly different ideas as to how many pieces it takes to make this fender, but Bruce decided on three pieces: one central, or main part of the fender, and two narrow sides, each of which will have wire reinforcement at the edges.

THE PATTERN

Bruce starts by making the pattern from paper. As you can see, the paper is clamped to the buck and the dirty-finger technique is used to mark the edges. Bruce cuts the paper just a little generously to ensure that we have enough material.

Once the paper pattern is trimmed to size, the outer edge will have to be cut longer than indicated so there is adequate metal to wrap around the wire. The material in this case is .160 inch diameter mild steel wire. Bruce goes so far as to wrap a piece of scrap material around the wire so we know how exactly how much metal to leave at the edge. Based on the test we need an additional .375 inches of aluminum sheet.

Once he's sure there's enough metal to make the fender side and wrap the wire at the edge, Bruce cuts the piece out of exactly the same material used for the main part of the fender.

SHAPING THE SIDE

After sanding the edges and annealing the entire piece Bruce holds the flat material up against the buck and forms a plan. The actual shaping starts with the small shrinker. As Bruce is fond of saying, "These small shrinker stretchers are extremely handy, look at how much shape we obtained in just one pass through the shrinker."

Next comes a session on the post dolly. "This is called working off dolly," explains Bruce. "I'm not hitting the metal right at the spot where the dolly is positioned underneath. I'm slapping it with a Covell slap hammer, off the peak of the dolly. This is a forming operation, no shrinking and no stretching."

Continued, page 121

With the center panel of the fender fitting the buck, it's time to start the side panels.

Establishing estimated shapes of side panels is done with the paper pattern technique.

The "ol" dirty finger trick still works to mark the edge of the pattern.

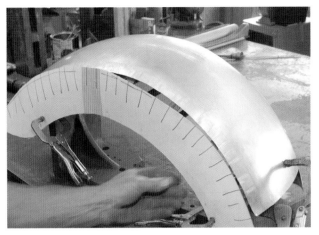

Slicing edges helps to determine desired shape.

Here the initial sidepiece is cut.

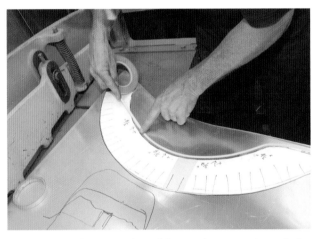

Here I'm indicating the additional material needed to allow material for the wire wrap.

Next I anneal the new side panel to make it easier to shape.

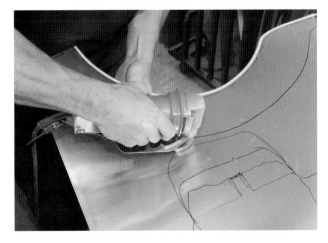

With the electric shears I cut positive 1/8 inch to ensure there's enough material

Always check and make the way your part fits the buck.

I like to take one last chance to consider how the side panel will fit before I begin shaping.

Covell's famous lightweight slap hammer is great for forming over a dolly as seen here.

A little shrinking on the edge starts the process.

Use a rounded post dolly to help maintain uniform contouring.

I'm always checking the fit on the buck.

Again, check the fit.

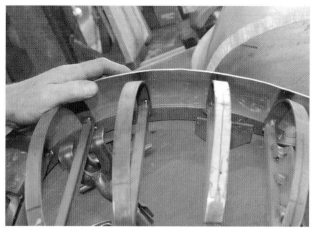

Also check the backside of the panel to see how tight it is against the buck.

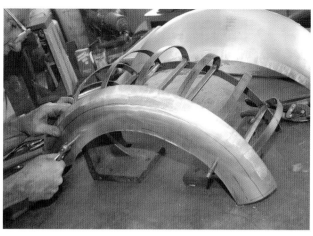

The side panel is looking pretty good, here you can see how the Clecos hold the panel against the buck.

A couple of 1/8 inch holes and 2 Cleco clamps ensures that the panel is in the same spot every time.

Top edge of panel is connecting well with the buck.

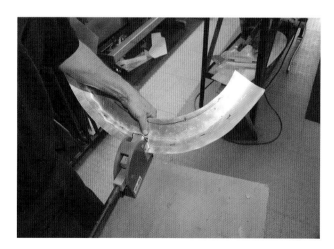

Now I'm heading to the outer edges with more shrinking.

Every cross section must fit tight against the panel.

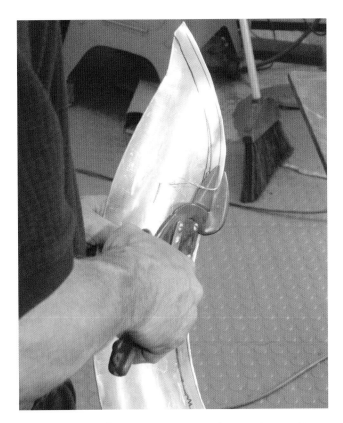

When I trim the piece I'm sure to leave 3/8 to 1/2 inch of material for the wire wrap.

CHECK TWICE, SHAPE ONCE

As always, Bruce checks the progress of the piece often against the buck. To make sure the fender side will be in the same place each time, Bruce drills a couple of holes for the cleco clamps. The fender isn't tight enough to the buck at the top where it meets the center part of the fender, so it's back to the shrinker for more shaping, followed by a little slap-hammer work (not shown), and another check against the buck. At this point, the fender side is fitting pretty well, and Bruce runs it through the English wheel to smooth out the highs and the lows.

As mentioned before, there is nothing worse than cutting yourself short, literally.

"The most important part of fabricating is to make sure you have enough material," says Bruce. "Never go negative, or you will have to weld on more material. It's like a steak, you can always go from rare to well done, but you can't go the other way. I like to wait until the part is nearly done before I cut off any excess, because the dimensions can change."

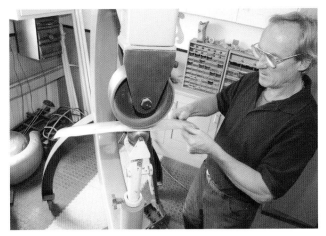

After shrinking, the English wheel helps smooth out the bumps.

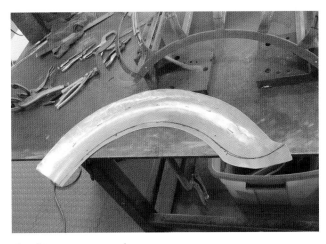

Looking pretty good.

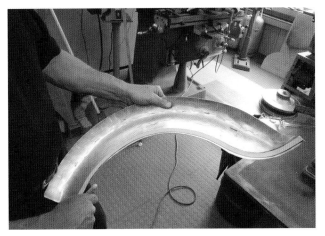

Refining the edges.

A progress shot, notice how nice the underside of the panel fits up against the buck.

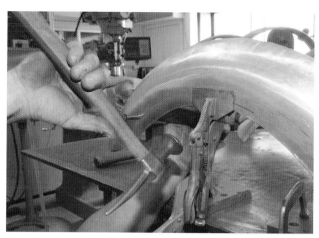

The first step: break out the most important tool, the large domed hammer.

With the panel a pretty good fit against the buck, I clamp it firmly in place before I begin to wrap the lower edge.

I use a smaller hammer for the details.

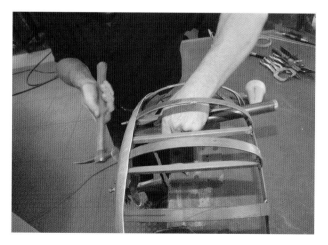

The edge of the buck is used to start forming the wire edge.

It's good to use a dolly to "back the part" when hammering the edge.

Having said all that, Bruce does cut off the excess, and then begins to roll the edge of the fender over the buck. The important thing is to make sure that the edge we roll over the buck is uniform all the way around.

For part of this rolling-over operation, Bruce uses a dolly or backing bar behind to, "add integrity to the edge as I beat on it. You can do this operation easily with the beading machine," says Bruce. But we are tying to do this the way a person at home would do it."

As shown, once the lower edge is rolled over, Bruce makes sure the fender side is positioned under the main fender before marking the edge. Once the edge is marked, Bruce trims the top of the fender side very carefully with a high quality tin snips.

WIRED

Bruce explains that, "You can put the wire in now, or put it in later after the side section is attached to the main fender, but it's easiest is to put the wire in now. It's good to have the wire

greased or painted. With most of the old cars it was just put it in there uncoated, but then they would rust. Galvanized wire would be good, but I don't know if you can buy it that way.

Bruce bends the wire over various round shapes until it matches the radius of the fender, then pinches it in position in the fender with a vice

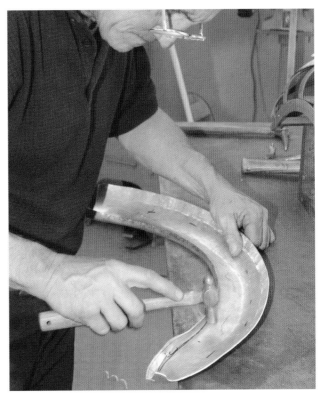

1. Before doing the final trim of the upper edge, I overlap the two panels, mark the edge, and the create witness marks.

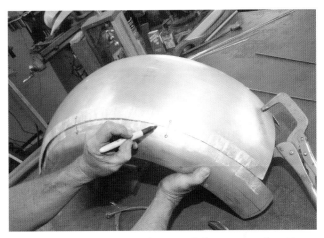

2. Now I can do the final trim by hand with a high quality snips.

3. Small details are worked out from the back side with a small hammer.

123

Here you can see the beginning of the edge that we formed with help from our working buck.

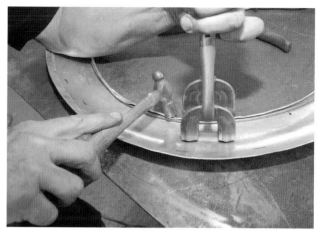

Now I can start clamping and hammering the wire in place.

You can rough shape the wire on any radius you find nearby.

A pinch here and there holds the wire in position.

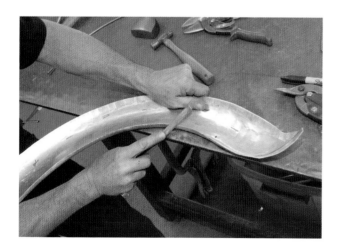

I like to file the rough edges by hand.

I close up the fold with the small hammer.

Here you can see the edge completely wired, it's time to start welding

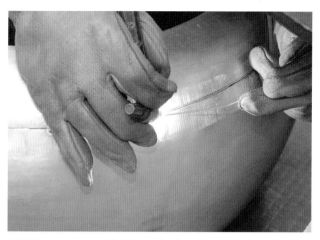

Welding time, I like to tack the seam every 1-1/4 inches with the TIG welder.

One final check for fit, being careful to align the witness marks.

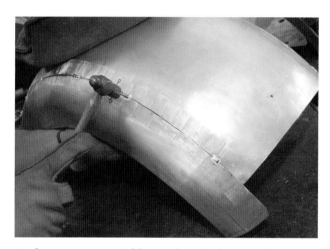

Before moving on I like to planish the seam lightly to ensure good alignment.

A little more trimming is needed as shown.

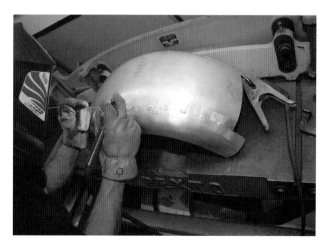

More tack welding with the TIG welder.

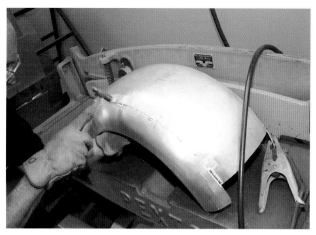

It's good to planish as you go, raising the lows and lowering the highs.

the is still a little work to do though, finishing the wire edge at the tail section.

Once the seam is nice and smooth, with good fitment between the two pieces of metal...

The hammer and buck are used to shape the edge of the flared tail section.

...it's time to finish the weld. Finally, the sides are welded completely to the center panel.

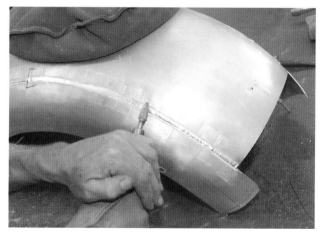

I begin the metal finishing by cutting the tops off the weld.

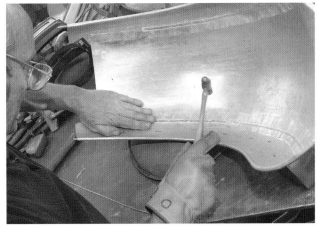

I do a little hand planishing on the backside of the seam, after the fusion welding.

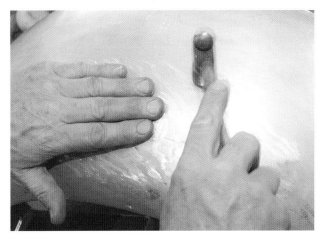

I'm using the hammer to raise the lows and knock down the high spots.

I start a little hand filing to see "what's up."

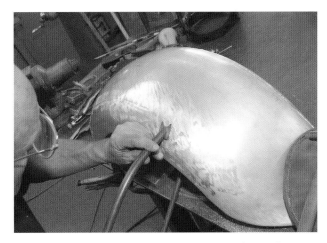

After planishing and filing a "swing pick" with a blunt tip is used to raise small low spots.

Here you can literally see what's up, and also what's down.

Final filing to perfection.

A 280 grit pad on the DA with WD-40 used as a lube removes evidence of the file work.

Steel wool and WD-40 does a nice job of fine finishing.

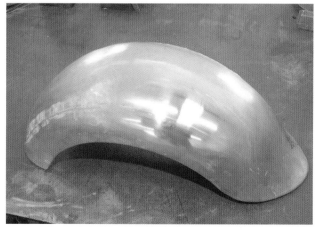

Here a mirror finish is created with absolutely no weld seam showing.

grips – note the nearby photos. Next, he starts to wrap the metal over the wire with a series of blows from a small hammer. Once the edge is rolled over the wire, it's time to double check the fit of the seam and then begin to tack weld the seam where the fender side meets the central part of the fender.

"On the TIG welder I use a sharp point on a 2% thoriated, tungsten," explains Bruce, "which is not how the pros tell you to do it, but it works very well for me. The non-thoriated tungstens form a ball and make a broader arc." The rod Bruce uses is number 1100, .060 inches in diameter, or the same thickness as the material. The welder is set on AC at 90 amps.

Bruce adjusts the seam with a hammer and dolly, to get the two edges to meet, both before and after the welding starts. After the initial tack welds, Bruce checks to ensure the two pieces of metal meet perfectly, before doing another series of stitches.

Once he has a stitch positioned about every inch or inch and a half, Bruce does one final series of edge adjustments, then runs a bead from one end of the seam to the other. Bruce fuse-welds the inside of the fender, using no filler rod.

The area where the new side panel meets the tail requires a little massaging, Once the wire is contained by both the fender side and the tail, it's time to finish all the welding.

METAL FINISHING

The initial finishing is done on the seam with an air grinder or zinger and an aggressive bit. Part of this demonstration is done on the other side, which has already been welded and is partly finished. The idea here is to show the various stages of finishing.

Some of the early work is done with the bull nose file, to which does a good job of showing the high and low spots. The surface is then adjusted with a hammer, followed by more filing.

Bruce moves the file at a 45 degree angle to the seam, as it takes off metal it shows the high and low spots. Once the low spots are identified it's a relatively easy mater to raise those, in some cases with the pick, as shown.

Captions by Bruce Terry

Q&A: Bruce Terry

Bruce, give us a little background, how long have you been a fabricator and how did you get started?

I've had my own fabricating business for about 20 years,

It started when I was working on vintage cars, basically when I get good at one thing I get bored. It got to the point where painting bored me. I always get intrigued by things I don't know how to do. So I started doing patch panels, learning how to butt weld them in place. Pretty soon the panels got bigger and bigger and as they got bigger they had to have some shape.

There was no one in those days to teach you, you just had to work on the metal to make it fit the space. Pretty soon I gave up the body shop and went to work for Thomas Kreed, that was strictly metal work. I went from the top of one profession to the bottom of the other.

It was a sacrifice, you have to have the passion to do this. There's a big learning curve in metal shaping. That's what I love, you never know it all. There's always a new challenge, that's the beauty of it. The exciting part is getting involved in projects that need creativity, hot rods and custom bikes and that kind of thing, so you mix creativity and the craft. I always say, 'there are people who are good craftsmen. Very few are really good artists.'

Tell us a little about the tools someone at home needs to do basic metal shaping?

To be reasonable, they need what we used. A good hammer and dolly set. With aluminum you can use carved hardwood, Grind the wood to the shape you want and beat the metal over that. You also need a leather hammer and some wood mallets and assorted T- dollies. The little shrinker-stretchers are pretty much critical, especially for the price. You don't need a break, you can bend it by hand with a hammer working over an edge.

For welding you should start with an oxy-acetylene torch, for a home shop that's the most bang for the buck. Learn how to weld with that. It also makes a softer weld for aluminum than a TIG does. A small MIG is nice if you have the money. You can have all that stuff for one thousand to fifteen hundred dollars.

The three tools you really need are patience, practice and persistence.

Any tips on learning the craft?

The books are good to help people understand the concepts. But you have to really be hands-on to learn to do something with the metal. Take a piece of metal and start shaping it. You need to understand the principles, the shrinking and stretching. You have to understand what's going on. Everything is just shrinking and stretching and breaking (bending). That's all there is. I'm self-taught. I beat on the metal until I learned how to make shapes. Everybody should start out forming parts by hand. To get a feel for it, 400 years ago they were doing swords and armor by hand.

What about materials, how do you decide whether to use steel or aluminum?

Well, shaping steel takes more energy, it's not as malleable. If it's a part that gets vibration you want steel. It's not that much harder to shape, especially if you get aluminum-killed steel. You need to apply the same techniques to steel as aluminum. Steel is generally more durable, and for most people it's easier to weld steel. If you learn oxy-acetylene welding and get good at planishing, that's a good skill. I would start on steel.

Why do people fail?

You have to be willing to invest the time, you have to pay your dues, it seems like people don't want to pay the dues. Guys who come to my seminars are blown away by what they can accomplish. If they're driven enough they can probably learn it. Motorcycles are smaller and have more shape so in some ways the parts are easier to shape. The most difficult parts to make are the flat things, like a hood. A hood is hard, or a door skin.

What's the most common mistake?

The worst thing you can do is over shape a piece. You can always put more shape in a panel, but you don't want to take shape out, that's a hard fix. If you don't check it all the time and you go too far. You might as well just throw it out and start over. Go slow and check your parts regularly. I like to tell my students to sneak up on it.

Get Tanked

No Buck, No Sketch

The sequence seen here documents the creation of a long, shapely motorcycle gas tank by Rob Roehl in the Donnie Smith Custom Cycles shop. The tank is part of a bike building project for what might be called a pro street model. A long and lean, hand built motorcycle with a 124 cubic inch S&S engine and a fat 300 series rear tire. Rob starts with the tank tunnel, then moves on to the top of the tank. The whole thing is created without a sketch or a buck.

Built by eye without a buck or a formal rendering, the finished tank is so shapely it could just sit on the shelf by itself like a piece of sculpture. Gold leaf scallops by Lenni at Krazy Kolors.

METAL WORK
Shape the Tank Top

After cutting out a piece of 16 gauge cold rolled steel, Rob uses the power hammer to do the initial shaping. "Basically I'm stretching the metal," explains Rob. Next, he moves to the English wheel, "I start with a pretty aggressive wheel on so it's going to raise the crown pretty fast. The wheel will also smooth out the lumps from the power hammer."

Next, he takes the top of the tank and shapes it by hand. Then it's back to the English wheel with a flatter, lower wheel. "I want to get more shape the short way so I change to a less aggressive wheel. The first wheel was so aggressive it almost left grooves in the metal so I'm using the flatter wheel running the short way to get rid of that and add some shape, pretty soon I will pull it out and evaluate my shape."

"Now I want to create a little more shape at the edges with the slap hammer and the dolly. I'm just trying to add shape, I can deal with the puckers later. The slap hammer is nice because it doesn't dent anything, and with the leather face, it doesn't even mark the metal."

Once Rob is finished rolling out the top, he trims it pretty much to size and tack welds it to the tunnel, which is already fabricated. "I don't finish weld till I'm right at the end," explains

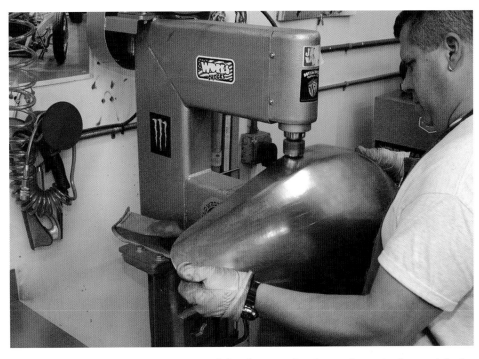

Most of the shaping for the tank top is done with the small power hammer.

This is essentially a stretching operation, more crown means more time spent on that area with the power hammer.

131

These are the basic stretching dies Rob uses for projects like the tank top (shrinking dies are available as well).

To raise the metal more the short way, Rob turns the top 90 degrees and begins a series of back and forth motions.

The English wheel is another stretching operation, one done by squeezing the metal between two wheels (note the photo on the next page).

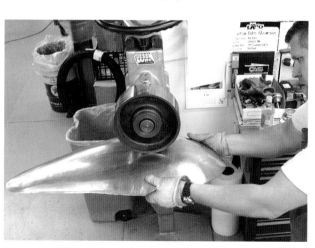

Rob patiently runs the tank top back and forth through the wheels to raise metal through the center of the tank.

A variety of lower wheels are available, this mildly crowned roller is Rob's choice for much of the early wheel work.

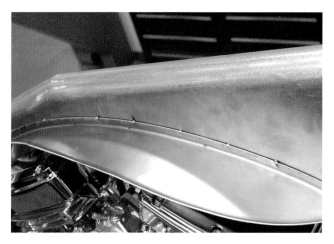

This close up shows the lip Rob put on the edge of the tank bottom, which adds strength to the edge and will prevent warpage when that seam is welded later.

Rob often uses the slap hammer to roll and edge.

It's important to take frequent breaks to evaluate the shape as it progresses.

The leather face on he slap hammer means the tool leaves the metal unmarked.

Sometimes there's no better tool than a strong back and a pair of willing hands.

Though it's a little hard to see, Rob has the top formed, as well as the tunnel, the two are tack-welded together. Time now to make the side panels...

...which start as pieces of light board cut to size...

...the panels are then cut out of 16 gauge steel, rolled out over a big piece of pipe for the initial shape and then run through the English wheel.

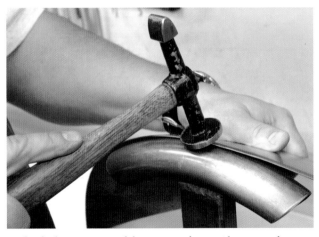

A body hammer and home-made anvil are used to roll the edges of the side panels.

Rob, "just a couple of little tacks will hold the top and tunnel together."

TANK SIDE PANELS

For the side panels, Rob takes poster board, makes templates and then cuts the panels out of steel. To do the initial shaping, Rob rolls the panel over a piece of pipe, then does a bit of work with the 'wheel. Not entirely happy with the shape, Rob rolls the edges with a hammer and dolly and then runs the panel through the wheel again.

Before welding the side panel to the top and bottom, Rob needs to trim it to size. "A lot of times I tape a panel to the other parts and then do the trimming, it means I don't have to have so many hands. Once the trimming is done, I'm going to work on the side seam, tack weld it, then drop out the tunnel and work at finishing the

With the help of a ruler, you can see how the side panel is crowned in both directions.

Now Rob starts to add more crown to the side panel by running it...

...through the English wheel.

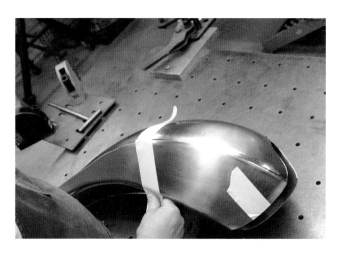

Before beginning to tack weld the tank together, Rob tapes the side panels in place.

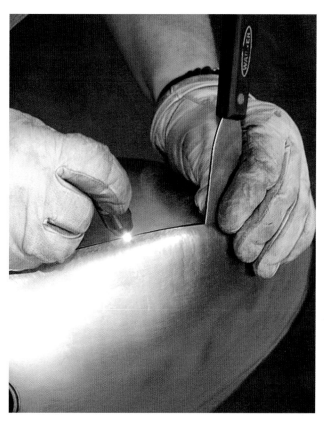

Note the way a putty knife is used to prevent one panel form sliding over or under the other, welder is set at 80 amps DC for the tack welding.

Rob does a bit of work on the seam as he moves along with the tack welding.

Rob uses just a few tacks to hold the panel in place, then assesses the fit before going any farther.

With no bottom, Rob can easily get at both sides of the seam and ensure that the seam is nice and smooth before finishing the rest of the tacks.

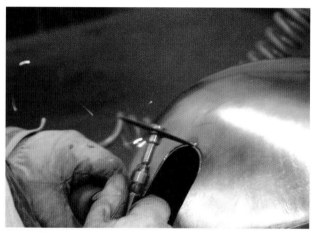

Because the tank top is held in place with just a few tack welds, Rob can cut those...

Tack welds are spaced evenly...

...and separate the two halves of the tank before proceeding.

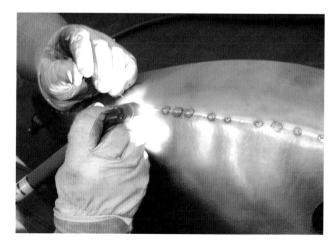

...down the side of the tank.

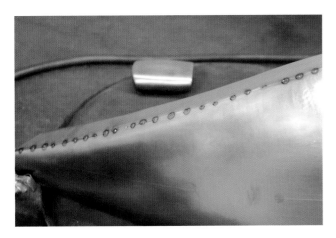

When he's done, Rob has a nice neat seam, with evenly spaced tack welds and no overlap where the two pieces of metal meet. And he can still get at both sides of the seam.

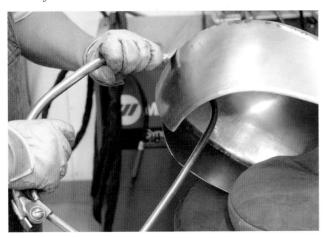

This is the bull's eye pick as described in the text, it's kind of a pick and dolly all in one, good for raising small areas.

The true beauty of Rob's plan is the ease with which he can get at the back side of the seam to correct a low spot before final welding begins.

seam. The bottom seam will be done last. The hardest part of making the side panels is getting them both the same."

TACK WELDING

"The most important thing to remember during the tacking process is to keep the joints butted together and not overlapped. I can close up the gaps later but if you overlap the joint you never get that out of it. The seam is so strong at that one point that you can't hammer it or shape it."

"At this point the bottom seam looks a little uneven but all that will pull in when I do the welding. Now I'm going to cut the tack welds and drop out the tunnel. Once I separate the top of the tank from the tunnel I can work both sides of the seam with hammer and dolly and slapper."

In one area the seam is low, so Rob rolls the top of the tank over and raises the metal from the back side. "Once I've got the seam pretty even I can come in and fill in some of my tacks."

There's a little overlap at the front of the seam, Rob tries the bull's eye pick, then a little work with a hammer working over a stationary dolly. "It raised the low part of the seam pretty well. If it had been any worse than this I would have had to cut the tack welds." The seam is looking pretty good now so Rob starts in on the final welding.

"I do an inch and a half of the seam, then stop, look at it, let it cool a little bit, and go back. I don't find much advantage in doing a lot of work on the seam with a hammer and dolly as I go. This seam has a lot of strength because of the shape, and I have it fitting pretty good right from the start, so I can just go over it with a small grinder later.

When the side seam is finished, Rob can weld the bottom, or tunnel, into the tank. As mentioned earlier, this seam is easier to weld without much warpage because both edges have a little shape right where they meet.

THE BOXED STRUCTURE

"I'm going to make this boxed structure under the top tube, which will help to stiffen the frame, and also give me a good place to put the front mount. In the rear I will use a regular T-mount."

The box is made from 1/8th inch plate. As

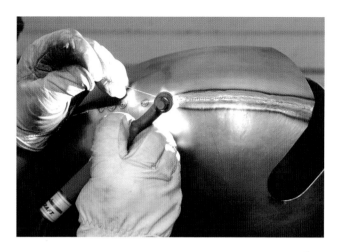

Rob does the final welding with 70 S2 rods, 1/16th inch diameter, "I pick the size of the rod by the gap I have to fill."

The final welding isn't done all at once, because too much heat would likely cause warpage. Instead, it's done in sections...

...with time to work the seam, and let it cool, in between welding.

In the hands of a craftsman, the tig welder leaves a very neat seam with a small heat-affected-zone.

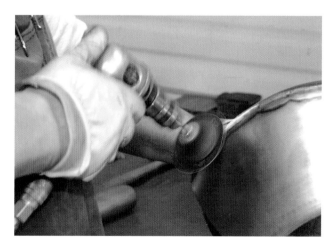

Though a heavier gauge of steel is harder to work, it also means Rob can use a sander on the seam without any danger of over-thinning the metal.

Welding in the bottom will be done now - after the side seams are fully finished.

The test fit shows a very nicely curved tank with all the lines converging at the back.

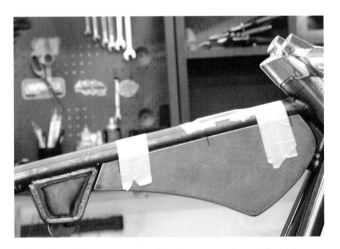

This boxed structure under the top tube will add strength to the frame and also form an external "bottom" to the gas tank.

Rob explains, "The boxed section also makes a very nice 'bottom' for the gas tank and gives it a nice finished look. The fitment of the box and tank are critical. I always spend a good bit of time fine tuning the position of the boxed section and the tank."

Now Rob tack welds the box to the top tube. Small panels still have to be added at the front of the box to close it in. Rob spends a lot of time ensuring the tank and the inner box line up exactly at the front of the tank before starting the final welding of the boxed section, As is usual, he does the welds in short stitches. After doing two stitches he uses the slap hammer to adjust the position of the box slightly and then goes back to welding.

The boxed structure is finished and adjusted slightly to match the bottom of the tank, the tank itself is ready for mounts. Note, the rear mount is already cut out, the photos show Rob cutting out the bottom of the tank where the front mount will be installed. After the holes are cut Rob does a test fit then trims the holes with a mini-belt sander. "This is also the optimum time to eliminate all the pieces and grit from the tank," explains Rob.

TANK MOUNTS

"I always weld the mounts in as one piece," explains Rob, "and then cut the center out later (note the photos page 141). That way the tank doesn't suck in and change dimension when I'm welding. I set the welder at about 125 amps, because these mounts are heavier, and then during the welding I concentrate the power on the heavier piece and feather it out into the sheet metal." The welding is done in sections, Rob works on one corner first, then lets it cool and switches to the opposite corner.

Rob lets the tank cool for a good 15 minutes before cutting out the center sections of the mounts. Once the center sections are cut out, the rough edges need to be trimmed (with the mini-belt grinder again) so they're flush with the sides of the tunnel. (These mount 'kits' are available from Donnie Smith)

It's interesting to note the way Rob uses the big magnets to position the tank so the seams are easy to get at, and the way he uses a small block of

139

After a little metal-finishing the tank needs very little filler.

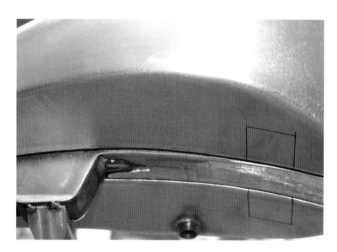

Happy with the fitment of the tank and boxed structure, Rob marks the location of the front tank mount.

The next task is to carefully cut along the outline of the mount with a cutoff wheel.

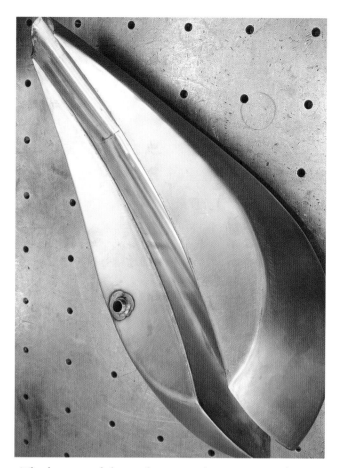

The bottom of the tank is every bit as nice as the top, so nice it's a shame to cut holes for the tank mounts.

steel as a rest for his hand. Note, the rubber pads, these regular softail tank cushions are used on the frame all through the process so the tank floats and isn't resting on the top tube.

With the frame mount screwed into place, Rob marks the boxed structure where it needs to be cut. "I'm just going to notch this with the cut-off wheel to match the thickness of the mount." Now the frame mount is screwed into place with the tank in place also, and two small wooden wedges are pushed into place to hold the tank centered on the boxed structure.

The frame mount is tack welded in place first, then the wedges are removed. Then the bolts are removed. What's left is final welding (the rubber cushions are removed before final welding) and the installation of the rear mount for the tank. "We usually wrap the upper tube with foam, that way it won't set up a buzz when the bike is running.

The bottom with the two mounts areas cut out and ready for mounts.

Welding starts with a tack weld at each corner.

But first Rob trims the holes for a perfect fit with his mini belt sander.

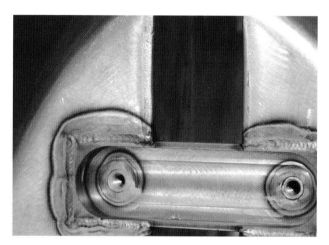

After the mount is welded in place as shown, and the tank has had a chance to cool off...

Before welding, note the nice flush fit and the minimal gap between the tank and the mounts.

...the center piece is cut out.

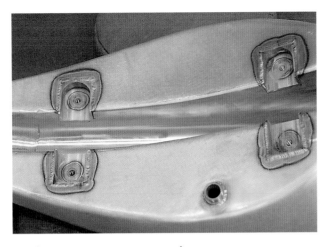

Both mounts are cut out in the center...

The tank is carefully positioned on the mount as described in the text.

...then the tank is dropped on again, and the frame part of the mount is screwed up into place and marked on the lower box structure.

Now the tank is lifted off and the mount can be final-welded to the frame (rubber mounts are taken off for the final welding sequence).

Now Rob does a cut out for the mount.

The finished tank, all of it formed by hand without a buck.

Q&A Rob Roehl

Rob Roehl is the long-time metal fabricator for custom-bike builder Donnie Smith. What follows are a few of the things Rob has learned during his career as a metal shaper.

Rob, can you give us a little background, explain where you got your training and experience?

I've worked for Donnie Smith for about 20 years, that's where I got most of my experience. Before that I helped my dad, who raced power boats. At that time you couldn't buy a lot of the stuff we needed so you had to make the parts.

How much of your work is building from scratch and how much of it is modifying existing parts?

I do both, 75% is building from scratch, the rest is modifying store-bought stuff. I'd rather fabricate from scratch if possible. Any time I can get a clean sheet of paper it's better than modifying something someone else built or designed.

What type of metal do you prefer to use?

I'm a steel guy, I do some aluminum, not much. For my application, motorcycles, it's the right material. Steel is durable, better for Harley-Davidson type bikes. Sometimes I prototype a part or design in aluminum, but not very often.

Do you always use a buck?

No, that's rare. Sometimes I just draw it out on cardboard or make a mock up. A lot of times I just make it. I am blessed with the ability to see things ahead of time and get them to look the way I saw them in my head.

What do you have for tools and what do you recommend for other shapers?

I've been a hammer and bag guy for years. I got the power hammer a few years ago. Hand hammering takes a toll on you. With the power hammer you can do it quicker with less wear and tear on the body. I've had my wheel for ten years and I use it all the time. That was built for my type of work, for what I do. Loren Richards built both my wheel and hammer. Unfortunately he doesn't want to make any more of those hammers.

I think the best way to learn is with a hammer and bag. You get that initial understanding before you start buying power tools. I did it for a long time without a power hammer. And I have to say the little hand shrinker/stretchers are great, even for a guy who's only doing this as a hobby.

How do you decide where to put the seams on big projects?

Seam location is dictated by how much shape you can put into a piece without making another piece. It revolves around your abilities to shape. If you can't deep-shrink you're going to have to cut and patch and weld.

What's your preference for welding?

You do what you do, what works best for you. I like TIG, it's clean. Wirefeed welders make a hard, dirty weld. I do it all heli-arc, but it's a skill that takes time to learn.

What kind of advice do you have for people starting out, or someone who wants to get better?

The advice I give to people is to be patient. Learn as much about metal shaping as you can and then just be patient. Practice, practice, practice. I look at stuff I did ten years ago and it's almost embarrassing, but it's all part of the learning curve.

If you stick with it you get a reward, like when one of my customers comes in and he sees the piece I've fabricated in the raw and it blows him away. He doesn't even want to paint it.

Rob Roehl, fabricator for Donnie Smith and very talented tin-man. Photo, Deb Shade

Classic Metal

From Original Rust to Better than New

The project seen here is the creation of two fenders for a 1922 Rolls Royce. Before the metal work can commence Craig Naff needs to make a buck and that's where this story really starts. Craig introduces us to this project by explaining how the old fender is used to make a buck for the new one. "To start I've set the old fender up the way it would sit on the car, then I draw a centerline front to rear and make a cutout that shows the outline of the fender, the profile or side view. I use that to

Old and new together. In back, the original 1922 Rolls Royce fender. In front, Craig's recreation. By using mirror image techniques one fender can be used to make a buck for both sides.

make the outline on the board that will run through the center of the buck. The buck itself is made from 1/2 inch particle board. I cut that center piece out with the jig saw or band saw."

For the next step Craig cuts a base for the buck explaining as he does, "I try to design a buck so I can reverse all the pieces and use it for the other side. It saves all the time of having to make that second buck." With the center piece screwed to the base Craig holds the original cardboard cut out up against the fender and marks a line where the fender lip meets the cardboard. Craig cuts a second template that matches the line of the fender lip exactly.

With the new cardboard pattern he marks and cuts out another piece of particle board that follows the fender lip. This new piece of particle board is screwed to the base, which was cut to be exactly the right width for this project.

Next Craig cuts out a template for the inside of the fender, along the rusty inner edge of the apron. A piece of tape shows where the actual edge of the metal falls, and where the top of the stepped section is. Craig follows the familiar pattern: create a cutout or pattern from cardboard, transfer those measurements to the particle board, then cut the particle board and mount it to the base.

Now the high point of the fender is marked at the very top. This reference point, 90 degrees to the centerline, is the high point of the fender when looked at front-to-rear. Craig carefully creates a template of the fender shape, in cross section, from the high point or center of the centerline to the inner edge, from cardboard. Craig also measures the distance from the centerline piece of the buck to the inner (front-to-rear) panel.

Now Craig installs the first of the side to side stations into the buck, even though this piece is not trimmed yet. The template made earlier from cardboard is used now, to mark the outline of the fender on the station just installed. Once the first station is trimmed Craig attaches it on three sides with more of the sheet rock screws.

To create the next station Craig makes another mark along the centerline on the top of the fender, then uses another piece of cardboard to create the

Craig starts the project by setting the fender up on the bench and then drawing out the front-to-rear centerline.

The next step is to make a cutout that follows the contour of the fender at the centerline.

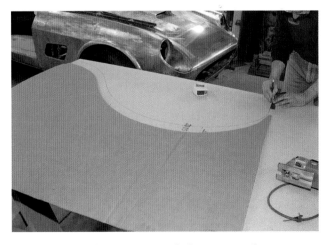

The cardboard cutout is used then to cut the center spine for the buck.

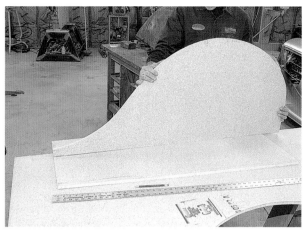

After deciding how wide the base should be, Craig locates the center piece, which will be held in place with sheet rock screws.

A separate piece of cardboard is used to fill in the outline of the fender lip at the rear.

Next, he makes a cutout of the fender lip...

The front-to-rear pieces are attached to the base with sheet rock screws. Craig drills holes in the base along the centerline of each piece.

...which is indexed to the fender itself.

The process continues as Craig makes another template, one that locates the inner edge of the fender.

second template for the second station. Like the first, Craig starts with a rectangle of particle board, then cuts the notch for the support on the inner side, then drills the holes for the sheet rock screws and mounts the new station in place temporarily. Now he traces the shape of the fender onto the station using the template created a few minutes earlier.

"I find that I don't use as many stations as some other fabricators," says Craig. "It's really a matter of personal taste. On this fender it's not changing shape very fast so I don't think you need as many stations. I tend to place them where there's a major shape change, so you would have the station at the highest point. The front station is positioned (note photo of fender profile) right where the curved shape of the fender changes and the radius becomes much tighter."

With that station in place it's time to measure down the centerline of the fender toward the front and create the location for the next station. The distance down the centerline is transferred to the centerline of the buck. Then the rectangular section is created. As before, Craig creates a cardboard profile of the fender at that station location, and transfers that shape to the station with a pencil, then cuts it with a jig saw. Any necessary trimming is done with a sanding block.

After the second station is cut and installed the process becomes repetitive. It turns out you have to be a bit of a carpenter to be a good metal fabricator. Working toward the rear of the fender the last station is placed where the fender changes shape, where it goes from a compound curve to a simple curve just before it meets the running board.

Craig explains that making the stations for the outside of the fender is done in much the same way as the inside, "I will use pretty much the same location (front to rear) for these but shift each one ahead or behind 3/4 inch to leave room for the screw heads."

The process starts at the highest part of the fender, Craig uses the same basic techniques seen earlier to build the stations. Each one starts as a rectangle of particle board, cut to slide between the center rib of the buck and the outside piece (the

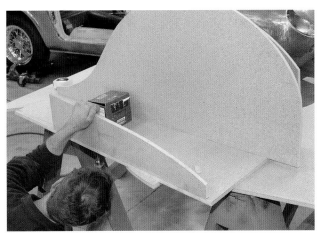

The baseboard is exactly the right width so the inner part of the buck goes up against the edge.

The first station will be positioned at the fender's highest point.

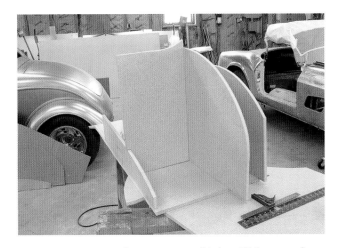

Here you can see the station - which will have to be removed again after Craig cuts a template of the fender's side-to-side contour.

147

Working at the highest point on the fender Craig makes a template that matches the shape exactly.

...before being reunited with the rest of the buck.

Then transfers that shape to the station..

Each station requires that Craig create a template of the shape.

...which is removed from the buck and cut along the contour line...

Then a station is installed in the buck at the same location.

Each station is first installed, then marked and cut along the contour line before being reinstalled.

And then the template made earlier is used to transfer the contour of the fender to the station.

After creating stations for the inside of the fender, Craig goes through the same process for the outside.

fender lip piece). After trimming and notching each rectangle it is screwed temporarily in place, then the contour or profile of the fender is transferred to the new station, it is removed, then cut along the line drawn from the template and reinstalled.

The final part of making the buck is to cut a big hole in the outside panel, "this is for access," explains Craig, "so I can see up inside the buck and tell whether or not the panel is sitting on the stations."

In this way and over the better part of a day, Craig creates a complete buck for the creation of the fender. "I don't hammer on these bucks," he adds, "That's a whole different process. I only use these for checking the shape." After trimming with a sanding block the buck is finished.

WHERE TO PUT THE SEAMS

When it comes to deciding where to put the seams Craig explains, "I try to split the areas with the most shape."Once he knows where the seams will be, Craig can measure along the centerline piece, then side to side, and transfer those dimensions to the raw sheet steel.

Craig only makes a paper pattern for certain

parts of the fender, "because the center part of the fender is a pretty regular shape I skip that pattern step. But I will make a pattern for the very front of the fender and some of the other areas too."

"The metal I use here is plain old steel. This is 18 gauge cold-rolled steel, it's all I've ever used. Ron Covell says to try the A-K but then I might get spoiled. And to get any of that material I'd probably have to buy a whole pallet. I use mostly power tools so it's not as critical to me as it might be for some other people."

After cutting the front corners off Craig washes the piece to eliminate the skin of oil and dust on the steel, and marks the line of demarcation separating the area of maximum shrinking from the rest of the panel.

Stations for the outside of the fender are staggered slightly from those on the inside.

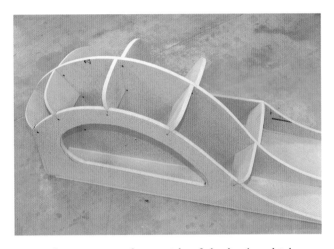

Note the cutout in the outside of the buck, which makes it easier to see up inside and ensure the metal is touching all the stations.

After the buck is finished Craig can begin laying out the panels and the location of each seam.

SHRINKING

Then he installs the shrinking dies in the Pullmax and starts in shrinking with thumbnail dies. Next Craig switches to the Eckold, explaining as he does, "The advantage of using the two machines is I can put gathering-type shrinking dies in the Eckold and smooth out the wrinkles left by the Pullmax while I'm still shrinking." Craig continues to work the edges, right up to and past the "line" drawn on the metal, with the Eckold.

Craig switches to the power hammer and stretching dies. "Now I have to bring the center up to get everything else to go down, if I continue to shrink it will just wrinkle up the edges."

TEST FIT

After that round of shrinking and stretching it's time for a test fit. "The only place it's touching the buck is in a narrow strip along the middle," explains Craig. "So if I raise the top more the sides will come down more until they touch the buck."

Now Craig goes back to the power hammer with the stretching dies. Then a test fit. The rate of change is slow now, the panel still doesn't wrap down enough at the edges. Craig marks an area in the center toward the back of the panel, that area needs to come up more, and then heads back for the power hammer. Another test fit, working along the transition area where it goes from stretching to shrinking.

Craig moves to the Eckold shrinker working mostly the edges followed by another test fit. What we see is lots of change from a small amount of shrinking. Another test fit shows the sides have come down considerably and the fit is much better.

Now Craig goes back to the Pettingell power hammer, explaining "We need dies that aren't so flat, so we can get out toward the curved area of the fender more."

At this point the project turns into a long series of test fits and power hammer sessions.

The test fit shows it to be over-shrunk a little, so Craig stretches it some along the edge again where it starts to turn down. Another test fit shows it to have lifted a little off the buck at the sides, but overall it's better. This test shows it to be rocking on the buck at the back in the center, so Craig stretches, or lifts it, in that area.

Rather than make a full paper pattern, Craig simply measures the width and length of the panel and cuts out a sheet of steel.

Craig makes 2 passes around the metal, going all the way to the edge of the shrinking area, then one more going about half that far in.

Paper patterns are used only for difficult areas like the very nose of the fender.

This is what the front of the fender looks like after the first round of shrinking with a thumbnail die in the Pullmax machine.

Craig starts the shaping process by shrinking all the way around the blank. Note the line that marks the edge of the shrinking area.

Frequent test fits are all part of the process and prevent Craig from going too far with one part of the fender.

Craig continues to shrink, but with a pair of gathering type dies in the Eckold. This way he can shrink and eliminate wrinkles at the same time.

Another test fit. The piece has come a long way in a short period of time.

The nose has a lot of shape and requires further shrinking.

We are getting close, after another test fit Craig declares, "it's fitting good at the front station but not too well farther back, so I'm going to raise that area to help the rest of it fit the buck. Part of the trouble is the way this fender rolls so much at the very front." The marks Craig makes on the fender are notes, telling him where to stretch and where to shrink.

He does just a little shrinking at either front corner, then more stretching, concentrating on a band running across the front of the fender. A test fit shows progress. The contour is coming along, though it's still off the stations some at the inside edge. Which means more stretching and more checking,

There's a tough-to-shape area between the first and second station on the inside where the fender goes from a lot of shape to an almost flat section as it makes the transition to the apron. Craig does a lot of fine tuning at this point, a little shrinking at the two front corners for example to get the tip to roll down more. Then more stretching all through the center of the piece.

After a break Craig starts the next session by installing a new lower die, one with a three inch radius, in the power hammer, explaining as he does, "I need to take the corner out of the curve on the outside, give it a more gradual curved shape." After working the area with the Pettingell it's time for another test fit.

Sometimes in areas where the edge doesn't come down far enough to meet the buck, Craig will stretch it, even though logic would suggest that the better way to do it is to shrink. "Sometimes I over-shrink an area and it will raise the area behind it, so then I have to go back and stretch it a little bit so the shrinking is relaxed and the raised area can come down." After doing exactly what is described above the outside of the fender matches the buck almost perfectly.

Craig changes to a six inch radius lower die because, "With the smaller die you really concentrate the power and move a lot of metal quickly." After a test fit Craig marks the areas that need to come up or be raised, then changes to a five inch radius followed by more power hammer work on the Pettingell. Then a little shrinking at the very nose and the corners of the fender to roll the tip down more.

This fender section is almost finished, Craig uses his hand to help identify high and low areas he can't pick up by eye. Again, he marks those areas with a red marker and then goes back to the power hammer for a little more stretching.

When the piece is done Craig takes it over to the planishing hammer. After applying a little spray lube the piece is run through between a pair of fairly flat dies to eliminate the hills and valleys in the metal's surface.

The planishing hammer does move metal, however, "just not as much or as fast as the power hammer." So Craig has to anticipate the metal's movement during the finishing stages. As an example he explains, "At our last fitting you could see the area in the middle needed to be raised more. But I left it low because I knew it would come up after we used the planishing hammer. Now the fit is pretty good, but the edges seem a little over-shrunk. That's OK though because those will relax a little after being run through the planishing hammer."

A good metal fabricator is forced to think ahead. It's not enough to get the shape perfect, you also have to consider the effects of the finishing operations on the contours you've created. Craig warns that you need to be careful when you're almost finished with a panel, "So you don't try to move the metal too far too fast, or you might be forced to start over. At the beginning of the project it's easier to correct for mistakes, near the end it's not."

Now a fairly crowned set of dies is installed and used to relax the outside edge and corner. The work on the outer edge with the more crowned dies caused the outside edge to relax and lay right down tight against the buck.

Now to the wheel, "to get some ripples out of the inside and also stretch that area just a little so it won't rock on the buck, and a little on the other side to smooth out the area with the sharp curve at the outside edge." All with moderate pressure on the wheel.

With a curved section like the outside edge, you have to use a planishing die with a lot of

Though the fender looks good so far, it's only touching the buck along a narrow center strip...

...the answer is to raise the center with stretching dies in the Pettingell power hammer.

By raising the center area the edges will come down closer to the buck.

153

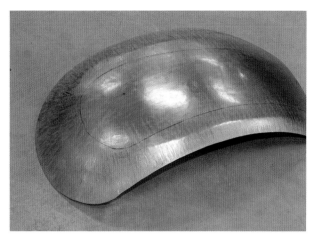

Though it looks pretty good the front of the fender still doesn't sit tight on all the stations.

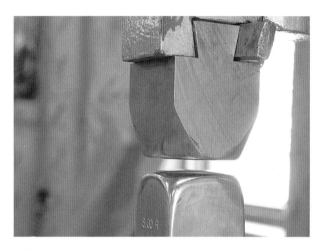

This lower die with an 8 inch radius is what Craig used for much of the stretching done through the center of the fender.

Here Craig works the transition area where the metal goes from stretched to shrunk.

crown. It is difficult to get a smooth finish with a high-crown die.

Craig declares the piece almost done, "the outer edge isn't quite finished but I've got to go in and add another piece to it later so there's no point in making it perfect right now." At this point the front edge has been left a little too long so there is enough metal to wrap a wire (a process that comes later).

THE NEXT PIECE OF THE PUZZLE

With the original paper pattern Craig checks the location of the side apron. With paper on the buck and pins in the places where the seam is located, Craig marks the edge, then transfers the measurements to the metal.

Now the newly cut piece of metal is held up against the buck and a line is marked that repre-

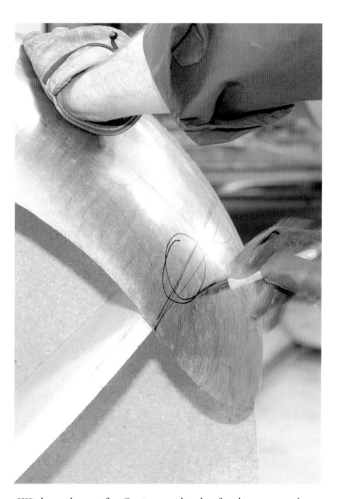

With each test fit Craig marks the fender as to what it needs and where. In this case what's needed is more stretching across the front...

sents the limit of the shrinking. The operation starts with the Pullmax, much as before, with the same dies. Craig follows the same procedure: first he makes two passes across the panel with the shrinker, going full depth each time, followed by another two that only go half way to the edge-of-shrinking line marked earlier.

The Eckold is next as Craig continues shrinking with the gathering-type dies. Note the dramatic and speedy way in which the big wrinkles are eliminated. This piece shapes fairly easily. Now he does a little power hammer work, using a die with an eight inch radius crown, which just happens to match the mild crown on the inside of the fender where it fades to the apron.

The piece is getting close, so Craig clamps it to the buck and then does a careful analysis of the progress. After making a few "notes" with red marker he goes back to the power hammer with the same eight inch die working the areas just marked.

ANOTHER TEST FIT

The part is not touching at the top, especially toward the front. Craig does a little shrinking along the edge and some stretching with the power hammer on areas that are touching the buck and holding the rest of the piece from fitting up tight. This process of getting the piece to lie up against all the surfaces of the buck involves many test fits and sessions with (mostly) the power hammer. At the end of the day the inner piece fits pretty well but it still isn't perfect.

One of the paper patterns Craig does use is a tracing from the front edge of the inner fender. Using this pattern Craig trims the panel at the front, commenting as he does, "I left about an extra inch so I'd have plenty of metal to wrap the edge wire."

A test fit shows the upper edge, especially toward the rear, rolls too quick. It's only hitting at the edge of the buck and not in the middle of the curve so Craig takes the piece over to the power hammer and stretches the metal in a band two inches from the edge. This relaxes the whole area, softens the curve and helps that area better match the contour of the buck. The same basic technique is used across much of the panel in order to soften

...done on the Pettingell with an 8 inch-radius lower die.

Another test fit shows the fender section as nearly finished, only a few problem areas remain.

Like the "corner" in the contour on the outside edge, which is smoothed out with a 3 inch-radius die.

At the end of the project the progress seems to slow down. The final fine-tuning includes raising the center of the fender with a 5 inch-radius die.

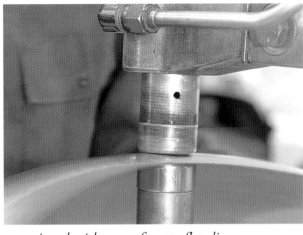

...equipped with a set of pretty flat dies.

To get the edges at the front to roll down more Craig does some additional shrinking.

The English wheel is used for two reasons: To smooth out imperfections left after the planishing...

The finishing starts with a few passes through the planishing hammer...

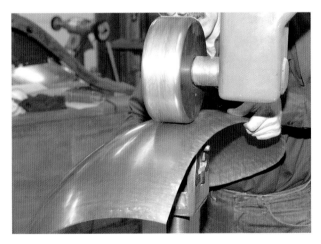

...and to stretch areas just in from the edge that need to be raised slightly.

the crown and help achieve a shape that matches the buck exactly.

Finally the inner panel fits all the stations except the one in the middle, causing Craig to comment, "it's fitting everywhere else so I'm going to let it go. The position of that one station might be off a little and we've got a nice smooth curve running across here and that's what you want. Sometimes you've got to trust your eye." Near the end Craig sharpens the radius at the very back of the panel by working it over a couple of dollies.

Time now to finish the panel. Once again Craig will anticipate the effects of finishing on the shape. It's still a little too tight overall and doesn't quite come up against the stations all across their surface, so if the finishing relaxes the panel just a little bit, that's fine.

The first step in finishing is done on the power hammer with a fairly flat die, one with an 18 inch radius. Next comes the planishing hammer and a few tweaks by hand until eventually the inner panel lays up against the buck the way it should.

Piece Number Three

Time now to make the third panel in this multi-panel project. Rather than make a paper template, Craig simply measures the distances on the buck and transfers those dimensions to the sheet steel.

He starts the shaping by hand, by simply bending the steel. Then Craig marks off various areas depending on which shaping techniques are required. Like the outside areas that need shrinking and the inside area, or crown, that requires stretching.

Craig begins the shaping on the Pullmax where the shrinking die makes quick work of the marked areas on either side. "I want to get this area to fit fairly well before I go to the other side, I don't want to get too far ahead of myself."

After doing the raw shrinking Craig moves to the Eckold to continue shrinking while smoothing out the lumpy surface left by the thumbnail die on the Pullmax. Craig stops before going too far, or the piece will be picked up right off the buck.

The fit of the front part of the fender on the buck is close enough that Craig decides to move on to the next piece.

When checked against the paper template the front of the fender proves to be a little long, but that's OK as we need extra metal for edge wiring.

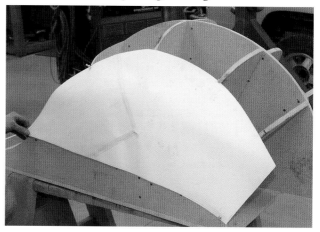

For the creation of the inner fender Craig does form a full paper template.

157

After cutting the mild steel sheet to the correct size Craig marks the limit of the area that he will shrink.

Here you can see in a series of steps...

Shrinking starts with the thumbnail dies in the Pullmax

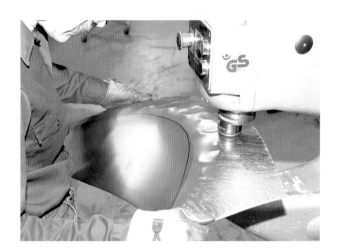

...how the Eckold is used again...

You can see how Craig made two passes, running the metal all the way to the marked edge of shrinking, then did another where he only went half way.

...to smooth out the ripples while adding to the crown.

After shrinking both the outside and inside Craig moves to the power hammer, with a five-inch-radius die, and works along the outside edge. This relaxes the edge on the outside rear and allows the panel to lie closer to the buck. The same procedure is used on the inside of the fender at the rear, to the same effect - the panel was a little over-shrunk prior to the power hammer work.

The next major step in the process is to stretch the metal all through the middle of the panel using the power hammer and the same die with a five inch radius.

After a test fit Craig continues with the Pettingell, stretching the center and smoothing out the transition from the softly crowned top to the more sharply curved sides.

More test fits and more stretching follow for a good 40 Minutes….

In a relatively short time the panel is essentially finished. Craig moves to the wheel to roll a nice transition area between the outer edge and the flat reverse-curve area at the back of the fender. "It works better than the hammer, which tends to leave the surface a series of flat sections."

Craig changes to a 10 inch radius die and uses it to raise the area just ahead of the reverse curve. This area between the two edges is now slightly concave and should be raised slightly. This is a difficult area to shape, as the metal in the center must go from crowned to a reverse curve.

A flatter wheel is installed and Craig works the rearward edge on the inside where the shrinking ends and the panel flattens out. This is very similar to what was done in the same area on the other side.

This panel is nearly finished. Craig stretches and shrinks small areas very carefully with many test fits and painstakingly gets the panel to sit on the buck and meet all the stations. At the end it's very much like a careful massage. Craig slides the edge of the metal between the shrinker jaws just long enough for a few gentle blows, then pulls it out for another test fit.

Where other fabricators seem to force the metal into submission, Craig encourages the metal to move.

Using a die with mild radius Craig begins stretching the inner fender or apron.

Next comes a test fit which shows the piece to be very nearly finished.

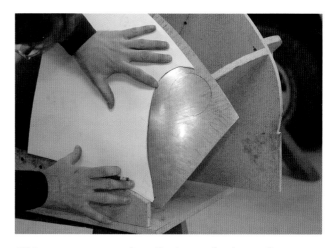

Using a paper template Craig marks the outline at the front of the inner fender, leaving a little extra metal for the edge-wiring that will come later.

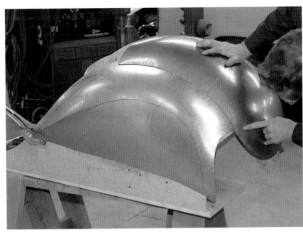

A test fit done with the front section shows the inner fender/apron to be touching at the top and front, but not in the middle.

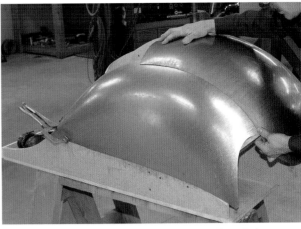

At this point the inner fender fits well, exhibits a nice shape, and blends well where it meets the front fender section.

The answer is to stretch the apron where it was shrunk earlier to raise and relax the area.

Time for piece number 3. .After cutting out the blank, shaping starts very much by hand.

Before declaring the piece finished Craig does a little detail work with hammer and dolly at the very back corner.

After the rough shape is established Craig does an analysis of the part and marks areas that need shrinking or stretching.

The hammer and dolly are used to eliminate some small dents at the back of the panel. Then Craig finishes shaping the end of the panel on the Eckold with a new set of dies, duralon upper and T-dolly lower, to roll the edge (see pics) then install stretching dies and stretch the same outer edge slightly. Now it is finally time for planishing and a little tweaking. Finishing this piece was made more difficult because of the transition area where the crowned center strip meets the flat reverse curve, with the crowned and shrunk areas on either side. Each little change in any one spot has profound consequences over a big area.

Craig attaches both front and rear panels to the buck to ensure they fit and fit together. He marks a line where they overlap and trims the upper piece nice and clean, then puts it back on the buck, "You have to be sure they meet nice and neat, I don't want to be stretching or shrinking that area afterward. When I'm trimming I bend the scrap piece up and out of the way as I go to minimize distortion of the main piece."

The two panels are joined by a series of tack welds, with hammer and dolly work after every couple of tacks. Craig does use filler rod for these tack welds. (.040, 70 S6 rod, with the welder set to DC straight polarity, 55 to 60 amps approximately).

Final welding is done in one inch strips, spaced out across the seam. After the four short bursts of welding, Craig hammer and dollys each one with a dolly that matches the contour of the fender. Then another series of one inch welds and another round of hammer and dolly work. In this way Craig works his way across the fender, creating a seam that is both strong and true to the overall shape of the fender.

Time now to join the side panel/apron to the rest of the fender. Before attaching the apron to the fender however, Craig cleans up the edge with a DA sander. After checking to ensure the transition area where the apron meets the fender edge is smooth, Craig decides to simply hold the apron in place and then scribe a line on the "fender." The cutting is done with a tin snips.

In a familiar pattern, Craig starts with shrinking in the Pullmax...

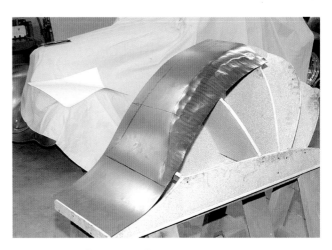

...and then does a test fit...

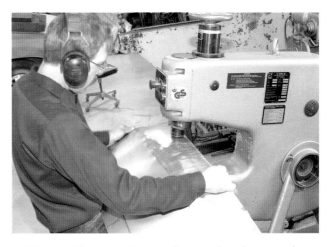

...followed by smoothing and more shrinking in the Eckold machine.

161

The test fit showed the need for more shrinking at the edge.

Time now to stretch and raise up the band of metal through the center.

Which must be smoothed out with the Eckold before...

Transition areas are difficult, like this area where the crowned areas meet the flat section on the back of the fender.

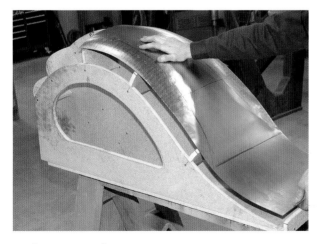

...the next test fit.

Off the buck the piece appears to be nearly finished.

After tack welding the finish welding begins. Again, Craig does a series of one inch welds, well spaced, with hammer and dolly work after every group of three or four. In this way he welds the entire seam from back to front with very little distortion. What's left is the installation of the outside panel and the edge wiring of the fender.

THE LAST PANEL

The edge wire used here is 3/16 inch mild steel rod. Craig combines edge wiring with the creation of the last, outside panel needed to complete the fender. As he explains, "It's much easier to put the edge-wire in place before the panel is shaped, rather than the other way around."

"The rule of thumb for edge wiring is: You need 2-1/2 times the diameter of the wire. In this case that's 15/32 of an inch from the edge."

Craig makes two marks, one at 15/32 and one at 3/16 of an inch from the edge, then uses those marks as guides as the strip of metal is placed in the break. The double bend forms a U channel, into which Craig slips the wire, which is initially trapped as Craig rolls the edge over with a body hammer.

To finish closing the metal around the wire he installs a special set of dies in the Pullmax and runs the edge of the fender through three times. The result is a very neat, clean edge wrapped tight around the wire.

After running the panel through the dies Craig starts the shaping by stretching the upper section first. The stretching causes the piece to form a definite curve. After a test fit Craig does another round of stretching before using the shrinking dies to encourage the metal to curve the other way at the back of the fender.

Some parts of the new panel pick up a little crown in cross section, "because the dies can only reach back as far as the wire." Craig eliminates the crown by running the piece through the planishing hammer.

Getting the panel to follow the outline of the fender is a matter of patiently stretching and shrinking with plenty of test fitting between. The long narrow shape of the panel means that it often picks up a twist during all this shrinking and

To create a nice rolled edge along the back of the fender Craig uses the English wheel.

To lift the area just ahead of the flat section Craig stretches the metal with the power hammer

To roll the inside edge Craig uses the wheel again, but with a different anvil wheel than was used on the other side.

At the end of the fender a special T-dolly lower, and soft upper, die are used to create a better rolled edge.

A test fit shows a good match between the three main panels of the fender.

Here you can see how nice the edge fits the buck.

With the panels trimmed and clamped carefully in place Craig can start to tack weld the three panels together.

The planishing hammer is used to finish the surface and do a little more stretching.

The tack welds are spaced carefully and cause no warpage of the panels or seam.

stretching. Craig eliminates the twist by simply hammering the piece flat on the bench.

The fact that we are trying to make the metal follow the edge of the buck points out the importance of making an accurate buck in the first place.

After the basic shape of the side panel is correct Craig needs to determine the exact shape of the front of the fender, because that edge must still be "wired" and the two panels have to come together smoothly. Craig uses a paper template to mark the new fender with the outline of the old.

Craig bends the front of the long panel until it starts to sweep over toward the center of the car, then clamps the panel in place, marks and trims away any excess metal. Dies in the Pullmax are used to create the mild crown on the new panel.

Craig scribes a line on the main fender now, then moves it to the bench and trims to the line with a tin snips. Next the outer strip is checked for fit and tack welded in place. The tacking starts at the front with a series of small fusion welds. For each weld Craig first moves the loose part of the fender around so the gap is tight, positions the welding tip close to the seam and then hits the gas. If the weld holds he readjusts the remaining strip of metal, does another fusion weld, and starts all over again.

Once the entire strip is attached with the small welds and the fitment is deemed good, Craig starts to do the final welding in short segments spread across the seam. The short weld segments produce very minimal warpage, the seams don't open up and they don't tighten up. One piece of metal isn't trying to jump up over another as a result of too much heat. The entire seam is welded up in this slow, patient fashion with hammer and dolly work after each series of welds is finished.

WIRED

At this point the front of the fender is pretty raw and needs a bit of massaging to create a nice accurate edge that encloses the wire. Finishing the fender edge starts as Craig wraps the wire behind the center of the fender and clamps it in place. Next, he scribes a line that represents the eventual end of the fender. Now Craig tack welds the wire to the two panels. despite the fact that there is con-

Final welding of the seam is done in one inch increments. After doing a series of these welds, Craig hammer and dollys the entire seam...

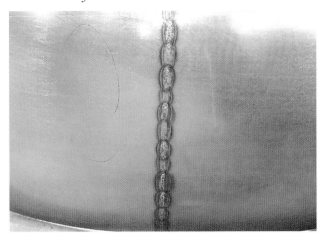

...then goes back and does another series of one inch welds.

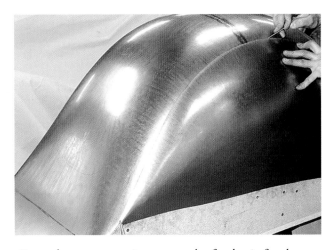

Once the seam running across the fender is final-welded, Craig scribes and trims the area where the inner fender meets the main fender.

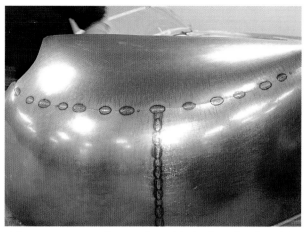

This seam too is first tack welded, then final-weld-ed in one inch strips.

For the outer lip Craig cuts a narrow strip of steel and a piece of edge wire just a little bit longer.

The ruler shows just how nice the seam is after final welding and a little hammer and dolly work.

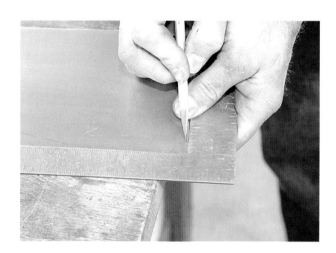

Craig makes two marks before placing the sheet of steel in the break...

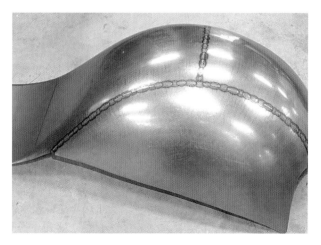

The fender appears finished, but only if you're look-ing at the inside.

...and carefully bending a neat U-shaped channel just big enough for the edge wire.

siderable overlap between the two panels (check the photos here to relieve confusion).

Craig heat shrinks the outside flap of metal, causing it to suck up tight against the main part of the fender. To cut out the overlapping metal, Craig uses a die cutter to create a cut, then inserts the blade from a powered keyhole saw. Now the new seam can be welded in the fashion illustrated earlier.

The tape line he runs across the front is just under 1/2 inch, or very close to 15/32 inch. Craig then trims to tape edge. Where there's not quite enough metal to have a full 15/32nd tab Craig welds a small extension on the edge of the metal. Now with just enough extra metal extending past the "end" of the fender Craig can enclose the wire.

With specially modified vise grips Craig bends a tab back a little past 90 degrees. This is done in a series of smaller steps working across the front and inside edge of the fender. With the fender flipped onto its side Craig now works the tab with hammer and dolly, gradually working it into more of a U shape.

After the U-channel is fully formed Craig cuts a piece of wire a little too long for the intended application. "Any unevenness you see along that edge can be eliminated when we put the wire in and fold the metal over the wire," explains Craig. "If you hold your hands well apart and bend the wire gently you get much nicer bends than if you put your hands close together and just muscle the wire." After being shaped the wire is clamped in place, marked where it meets the other wire (which was trimmed earlier) and then the two wires are welded together. This must be done without any build up or it will affect how neatly the sheet metal can be rolled over the wire.

Craig starts with the vise grip, folding the metal over enough to hold the wire in place, then comes the hammer and dolly. Once he has one area full wrapped around the wire he just continues down the wire.

If the piece is too big to go into the Pullmax the final crimp must be done with a specially mod-ified vise grip working from one end of the wire to the other. Now it's time to cut off the excess wire and declare the fender finished.

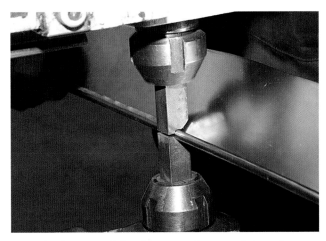

Final "closing" of the sheet metal around the edge wire is done with this special tooling in the Pullmax...

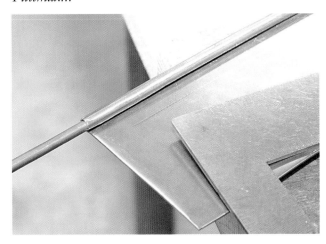

...which leaves the edge of the fender with a very nice "factory" finish.

The shaping starts after the installation of the wire - in this case by stretching the upper edge which quick-ly puts a curve in the narrow panel.

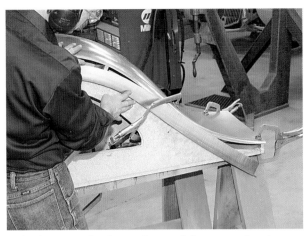

The first test fit shows the need for more shaping, especially toward the rear of the fender.

Because the wire will run all the way across the fender, Craig plans the "wiring" of both the inner fender...

Craig installs shrinking dies in the Eckold and shrinks the end of the fender-edge...

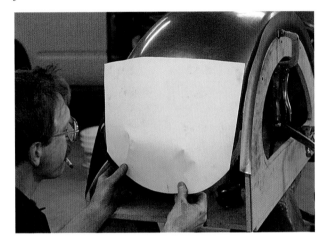

...and the fender tip, with templates made from the original fender.

...which causes it to turn up and follow the rest of the fender.

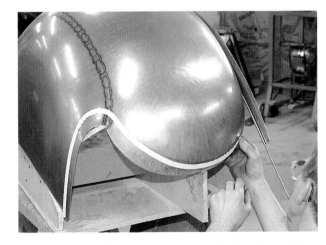

Here a piece of tape is used to mark the edge of the fender, leaving enough extra metal to wrap around the wire.

CRAIG NAFF INTERVIEW

Since making the move from conventional body work to metal fabrication twenty some years ago, Craig Naff has done a wide variety of work. From CadZZilla built in the Boyd Coddington shop for Billy Gibbons to the 32 Chevrolet cover car built by Larry Erickson (who designed CadZZilla by the way) Craig Naff has built everything from high dollar hot rods to restoration parts for old classics.

Like most metal working shops, Craig Naff's is crowded with cars and projects in various states of completion. Unlike a lot of shops, Craig's is very neat and contains both classics and hot rods. Near the door sits a Ferrari in bare metal, ready to go back to the nearby specialty shop for assembly, while a small group of hot rods occupy the remaining floor space.

Among the hot rods is a roadster with the lines of a 33 Ford. The car is Craig's creation, from the chassis to the body and running boards. The only part of the body that Craig didn't fabricate from scratch is a small section of quarter panel on either rear corner. As if it weren't enough to build a complete body and chassis, Craig also designed and built the dash, including the instrument cluster and convex glass dome. Even the taillight housings and lenses are Craig's design and fabrication.

When it comes to shaping sheet metal and fabricating parts, it doesn't appear there are very many things that Craig Naff can't do.

Craig, can we start with some background on you and how you came to be a metal shaper?

I started with auto body classes in high school. After that I worked at a Ford dealership body shop. Then I worked for White Post Restoration near Winchester, Virginia from 1979 to 1983. When I worked there the body people were responsible for all the body work on a particular car. That included the metal fabrication. But the shop owner liked my metal work and pretty soon he had me doing all the metal work. I just self taught myself the trade as I did more and more metal work.

By 1984 I was married to Kathy and working out of my own shop in Asheboro, North Carolina. I built a car there that won the Grand National

Getting the fender edge into precisely the right shape requires a certain amount of good old-fashioned hand work.

After scribing a line on the the fender edge where it meets the rest of the fender, the excess metal is trimmed away.

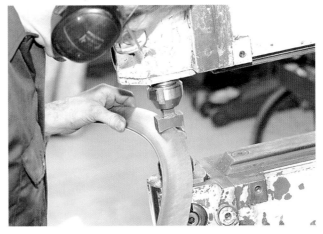

To create a soft crown in the narrow strip of metal, Craig uses a set of dies with exactly that radius, in the Pullmax.

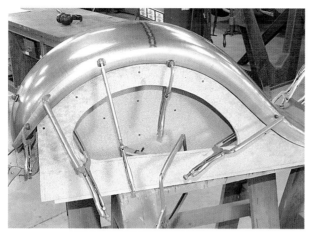

Once it's trimmed and shaped, the fender edge can be clamped in place. There is still an overlap where the two surfaces overlap...

As before, the finish welding is done in one-inch increments. Note how nice and tight the gap is - after the welding.

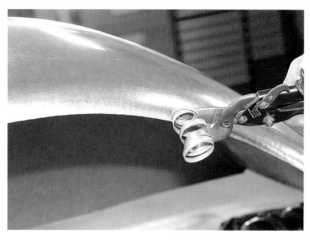

...so Craig scribes a line and carefully trims away the excess metal.

The nearly finished fender, missing only the edge wiring at the front tip and a bit of finishing.

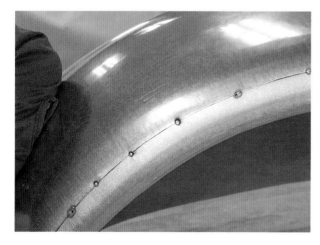

Once a nice clean butt-joint is established, it's time to tack weld the two pieces together.

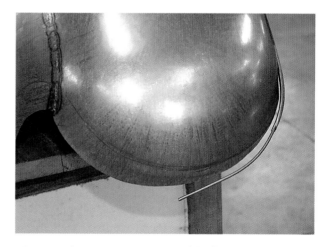

Getting the wire to run smoothly from the fender edge across the tip requires patience and a lot of hand work.

award at the Hot Rod Nationals in 1984. Boyd Coddington saw that car and pretty soon he started calling. Six weeks later we decided to go to California and work for Boyd. That was in 1986. We stayed there until 1989 when Kathy and I moved back to Virginia.

Once I moved here I did some Ferrari work. The first one required 75 percent new panels. Today I do both hot rods and restoration work, about 75 percent hot rods and custom motorcycles with the remainder being restoration work. I even do a little architectural metal work.

Which do you prefer, hot rod or restoration work and why?

I prefer the hot rods because of the creative element. There is always some design interpretation.

Is it necessary to have a good eye in order to be a good metal fabricator?

I think it is. Even when you're working from an accurate part, you still may need to interpret the shape because the original part is damaged or in poor condition.

Advanced Sheet metal means bigger more complex shapes. Can you talk about the seams. How does a person decide where to put the seams and how does he or she decide how many pieces to make an individual part out of?

As far as size, it's determined by the size you are comfortable handling, or the capacity of the equipment. Seams can be determined by the shape of the part itself. Often I try to divide a shape so you don't have to do all the shaping on one panel, to make the project more manageable and the panels easier to shape.

The Rolls Royce fender was made through a combination of shrinking and stretching. Do you try to use each technique in equal amounts or does it depend on the project?

Well, it's harder to shrink so I tend to stretch more. But you can't do so much stretching that you over-thin the metal.

Let's talk about welding. Bigger pieces mean more seams, how important is welding to sheet metal fabrication and is a TIG welder essential?

Welding is extremely important. You want to create minimal distortion. A TIG welder is essential

At this point Craig wraps the wire behind the fender tip...

...clamps it in place and scribes a line that represents what will be the edge of the finished fender.

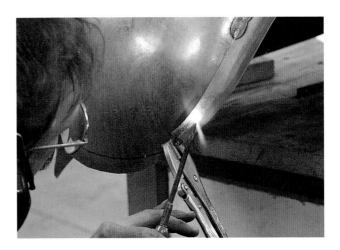

To get the strip from the narrow fender edge to pull up tight against the rest of the fender, Craig heat-shrinks just that area.

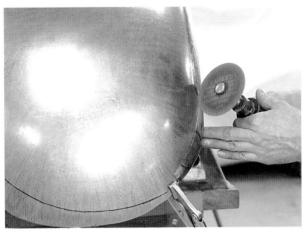

Metal from the fender edge that overlaps the main fender is trimmed away with the cut-off saw.

Forming a U-channel across the front of the fender is done by hand. The process starts as Craig bends the metal back with a modified Vise Grips.

Then a powered keyhole saw is used to cut a nice neat seam between the two pieces.

To finish forming the U-channel Craig uses a hammer and dolly with just the right shape.

After welding up the seam Craig runs tape across the fender to mark both the cut-off point and the eventual edge of the finished fender.

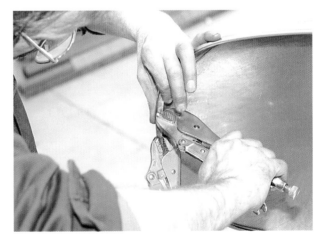

More vise grips are used to hold everything in place and begin closing the metal over the wire.

to me, I don't like MIG welds. I like gas better than MIG. MIG leaves lots of weld build-up. The welds are brittle and hard to work with.. You have more precise control with the TIG welder.

Concerning aluminum and steel, do you prefer one over the other or does the project determine the metal?

For fenders I prefer steel for the durability. They don't get dinged-up by gravel. Otherwise I don't have much preference. With aluminum you have to compensate for the lack of strength in engineering the part.

Is there one skill or ability that's more important than all the others when it comes to sheet metal fabrication?

They all have to work together so I can't say one is more important than another.

Tools, what is it about power tools that you like?

Partly speed, partly the fact that they're less physically demanding and not as hard on your body.

What does a young person need to get started on a career as a metal shaper?

Patience.

Tight corners like this require the use of a hammer to roll the edge over the wire...

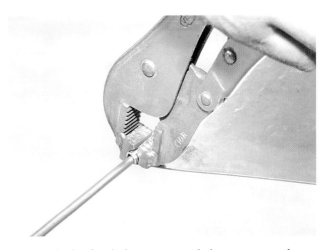

...though the final closing around the wire must be done by hand using another home-made tool.

Any further finishing will be left to the body and paint shop - at this point Craig declares the fender finished.

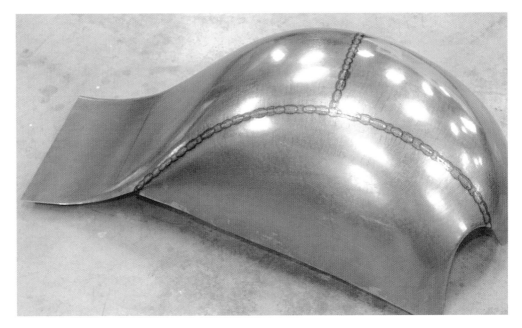

More Great Books From Wolfgang Publications!

http://www.wolfpub.com

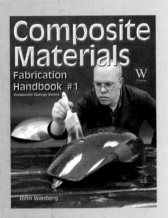

COMPOSITE MATERIALS FABRICATION HANDBOOK #1

While most books on composites approach the subject from a very technical standpoint, Book #1 presents practical, hands-on information about these versatile materials. From explanations of what a composite is, to demonstrations on how to actually utilize them in various projects, this book provides a simple, concise perspective on molding and finishing techniques to empower even the most apprehensive beginner.

Topics include: What is a composite, why use composites, general composite types and where composites are typically used. This book includes shop set up, design and a number of hands-on start-to-finish projects documented with photographs.

Surface sanding and finishing makes up an entire chapter, ensuring that the parts you manufacture are not only light and extremely strong, but also good looking as well.

Fifteen Chapters   144 Pages $27.95   Over 500 photos, 100% color

HOW TO BUILD A CHEAP CHOPPER

Choppers don't have to cost $30,000. In fact, a chopper built from the right parts can be assembled for as little as $5,000. How to Build a Cheap Chopper documents the construction of 4 inexpensive choppers with complete start-to-finish sequences photographed in the shops of Donnie Smith, Brian Klock and Dave Perewitz.

Least expensive is the metric chopper, based on a Japanese 4-cylinder engine and transmission installed

in a hardtail frame. Next up, price wise, are 2 bikes built using Buell/Sportster drivetrains. The recipe here is simple; combine one used Buell or Sportster with a hardtail frame for an almost instant chopper. The big twin chopper is the least cheap of the 4, yet it's still far less expensive than most bikes built today. Cheap Chopper uses 144 pages and over 400 color images to completely explain each assembly.

Eleven Chapters   144 Pages $27.95   Over 400 photos, 100% color

ADVANCED CUSTOM PAINTING TECHNIQUES

From legendary painter Jon Kosmoski comes the book: Advanced Custom Painting Techniques. Over 350 photos by well-known photographer Tim Remus bring to life Jon's explanations of panel preparation, gun control, kandy application, use of color-change materials, new metallic basecoats, and how to design and tapeout complex layouts.

Whether your painting projects ride on two wheels or four, this how-to book from Jon Kosmoski is sure to answer your questions. Four start-to-finish sequences take you into Jon's shop and illustrate each step in the process. 100% color, 144 pages.

Ten Chapters   144 Pages $27.95   Over 350 photos, 100% color

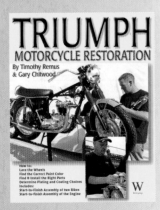

TRIUMPH MOTORCYCLE RESTORATION

As popular as the Triumph Twins were in the 60s and 70s, they are quite possibly more popular now. This book from Wolfgang Publications offers complete start-to-finish assembly and restoration sequences on two Triumph Twins, a 1963 Bonneville and a 1969 Bonneville. Also included is the start-to-finish assembly of the 1969 engine and transmission. Rather than try to describe the minis-

cule differences that often separated one year from another, this book offers a color gallery with left and right side views of all significant models from 1959 to 1970. With over 450 color photos, Triumph Restoration offers 144 pages of hard-core how-to help for anyone who wants to repair or restore their own Triumph twin.

Seven Chapters   144 Pages $29.95   Over 500 photos, 100% color

Wolfgang Publication Titles

For a current list visit our website at www.wolfpub.com

ILLUSTRATED HISTORY

Triumph Motorcycles | $32.95

BIKER BASICS

Sheet Metal Fabrication | $27.95
How to FIX American V-Twin MC | $27.95

COMPOSITE GARAGE

Composite Materials Handbook #1 | $27.95

HOP-UP EXPERT

How to Hop &
Customize Your Bagger | $27.95
How to Hop &
Customize Your Softail | $27.95

OLD SKOOL SKILLS

Barris: Grilles, Scoops, Fins and
Frenching (Vol. 2) | $24.95
Barris: Flames Scallops,
Paneling and Striping (Vol. 4) | $24.95

HOT ROD BASICS

How to Air Condition Your Hot Rod | $27.95
How to Chop Tops | $24.95
How to Wire your Hot Rod | $27.95

MOTORCYCLE RESTORATION SERIES

Triumph Resotoration - Unit 650cc | $29.95
Triumph MC Restoration Pre-Unit | $29.95
Harley-Davidson
Panhead Restoration | $34.95

AIR SKOOL SKILLS

How Airbrushes Work | $27.95
How to Airbrush Pin-Ups | $27.95
Air Brushing 101 | $27.95
Airbrush Bible | $27.95

PAINT EXPERT

Advanced Custom Motorcycle Painting | $27.95
Advanced Airbrush Art | $27.95
Advanced Custom
  Painting Techniques | $27.95
Advanced Pinstripe Art | $27.95
Kustom Painting Secrets | $19.95
Custom Paint & Graphics | $27.95
Pro Airbrush Techniques | $27.95

SHEET METAL

Advanced Sheet Metal Fabrication | $27.95
Ultimate Sheet Metal Fabrication | $24.95

CUSTOM BUILDER SERIES

Advanced Custom Motorcycle Wiring | $27.95
Advanced Custom Motorcycle
  Assembly & Fabrication | $27.95
Advanced Custom Motorcycle Chassis | $27.95
How to Build a Cheap Chopper | $27.95
How to Build a Chopper | $27.95

TATTOO U Series

Body Painting | $27.95
Tattoo- From Idea to Ink | $27.95
Tattoos Behind the Needle | $27.95
Advanced Tattoo Art | $27.95
Tattoo Bible Book One | $27.95
Tattoo Bible Book Two | $27.95

HOME SHOP

How to Paint Tractors & Trucks | $27.95

NOTEWORTHY

Guitar Building Basics
Acoustic Assembly at Home | $27.95

Sources

Rob Roehl
c/o Donnie Smith Custom Cycles
10594 Raddison Rd. NE
Blaine, MN 55449

Covell Creative Metalworking
106 Airport Blvd, Unit 105
Freedom CA 95019
800-747-4631
831-768-0705

Neal's Custom Metal
3023 104th Lane NE
Blaine, MN 55449
651-270-8410

Creative Metal Works
www.creativemetalworks.net
763-784-2997

Mike Pavletic Metal Shaping
12885 21st St.
Beach Park, IL 55449
www.pavleticmetalshaping.com
Mike@pavleticmetalshaping.com

Bruce Terry
Specialty Metal Fabrication
517 Airport Way, Unit M.
Monterey, CA 93940
www.specialtymetalfabrication.com

Craig Naff
1199 Stultz Gap Road
Woodstsock, VA. 22664
540-459-3394

Clay Cook
606-282-7545

Cal Davis
Metal Craft Tools
431 Linda St.
Macclenny, FL 32063
904-259-4427
Various tools and kits including power hammer
and English wheel kits.

www.metalshapers.org — Great source of ideas
and help from a wide variety of well-known
names in metal shaping.